THE COLLINS

BALLET
AND
DANCE
S T O R I E S

This collection first published in Great Britain by Collins 1996
Collins is an imprint of HarperCollins*Publishers* Ltd,
77-85 Fulham Palace Road, Hammersmith, London W6 8JB

1 3 5 7 9 10 8 6 4 2

The Stuff that Dreams are Made Of © Jean Ure 1996
Closer than Most © Sandy Asher 1996
Olé © Adèle Geras 1996
The Ghost of a Chance © Jean Richardson 1996
A Pair of Flat Feet © Alison Leonard 1996
Cécile © Rachel Leyshon 1996
Flair © Alison Prince 1996
Dancing Nancy © Josephine Feeney 1996
Jeffrey © Lynne Reid Banks 1996
Curtain Call © Jean Ure 1996

Illustrations © Rosemary Woods 1996

ISBN HB 0 00 185636 7
ISBN PB 0 00 675146 6

The authors and illustrator assert the moral right
to be identified as the authors of this work,

Printed and bound in Great Britain by
Caledonian International Book Manufacturing Ltd,
Glasgow G64

THE COLLINS BOOK OF
BALLET
AND
DANCE
STORIES

Edited by
JEAN URE

Illustrated by
Rosemary Woods

Collins

An imprint of HarperCollinsPublishers

Also by Jean Ure

For older readers
Skinny Melon and Me

For younger readers
Help! It's Harriet
Harriet Strikes Again

Contents

FOREWORD

It is my pleasure to welcome you to this collection of stories of dancers and dancing; a book about a world that has been *my* world for as long as I can remember. There has never been a time when I have not wanted to dance, and I can identify so strongly with the young people in these tales for whom that desire is equally passionate.

It takes all that desire, and more, to succeed in an art which demands so much dedication and perseverance. The path to the top is rarely straightforward. For every dancer, like me, who is fortunate enough to make dancing her profession, there are many more who are not so lucky. Disappointment and frustration are just as much a part of my world as success and applause, and one tries to cope equally well in both situations.

But dancing, I have always found, is its own reward. It gives back so much, whatever the level of participation. So often in this book, as in life, it is Mum who offers the right advice and puts things into perspective: "I just wanted you to have the experience of it," says Tashi's mother in Alison Prince's story, *Flair*. For me, this is what really matters, that everyone should have the chance to experience dance, whether or not their future lies on the stage.

I hope this book of stories will open the door to that experience and give you a glimpse into my world, so that you may share with me the pleasures within.

Deborah Bull
Principal Dancer
The Royal Ballet

INTRODUCTION

These ten stories have all been written specially for the *Collins Book of Ballet and Dance*.

When I asked my fellow writers if they would care to contribute, this is what I told them I was looking for: stories which encompass the desperate longings of all those girls (or boys) who aspire to become dancers. Stories which portray the glamour and excitement of the dancing world, and stories, also, which tell of the blood and the tears, the rose-pink, starry-eyed intensity, along with the inevitable hard grind and suffering.

So here they are! Ten stories all different, but all celebrating the joys, sometimes the pains, but always and for ever the sheer *magic* of the dance. They are about young people striving to succeed in their chosen discipline. Some of them make it; some of them don't. But all of them share the same passion.

Sandy Asher's *Closer Than Most* is set in America. Who's surprised when the rich mommy and daddy of new student Betsy automatically expect her to be given a solo in the annual production of *The Nutcracker* without even having to audition? That's the way of the world. For the talented Amy, the unfairness of it all ruins everything.

"Ballet has always been the one perfect thing in our lives...now it's all spoilt with...money, and selfishness, and cruelty."

But as her teacher says, it's easy to love something you

believe is perfect. The challenge is to go on loving it even when you realise it's not. That's the test of a real dancer.

In Adèle Geras's *Olé*, eleven-year-old Dympna comes to the sad realisation that she is simply "the wrong shape" to be a ballet dancer. She could still take lessons just for fun ... but with Dympna it is all or nothing.

"I'll never dance again," she said aloud, and noticed that her eyes had filled with tears and that a couple of them had actually begun to slide down her cheeks.

But Dympna finds she cannot live without dancing ... even if it is dancing of a different kind. Jean Richardson's Charley, in *The Ghost of a Chance*, is aiming high. She wants to go to ballet school as a full-time student. But is she good enough? As she confides her thoughts to her diary, other, mysterious entries begin to appear.

I'm going to LONDON! read the entry for 27 July. To audition for the SW school ... If I get a place, it will mean they think I've got talent.

Charley begins to feel a strange kinship with the ghostly diary-writer. It is as if their destinies are in some way linked. But will they both make it?

In Alison Leonard's *A Pair of Flat Feet*, Tom has been accepted as a dance student by the prestigious Drummond School, and is rightly proud of it. But during the day he has to attend an ordinary comprehensive school, and Bobby Hamilton, the class yob, has his suspicions...

"Saw these poofters in town Saturday," he said. "From the top of a bus... there was one of them the spittin' image of ye, Tommy."

Prejudice lingers on. Even today it takes more than just talent and hard work for a boy to become a dancer.

Cécile, by Rachel Leyshon, tells of the frustrations of a young girl at the Court of the Sun King in seventeenth century Paris. Cécile longs to dance. She is every bit as good as her friend Louis, but it is he who goes on to become celebrated, while Cécile must learn to know her place.

"*Young ladies of your upbringing,*" said Cécile's papa, "*do not parade themselves on stage for all and sundry to see.*"

Tashi, in Alison Prince's *Flair*, is dedicated almost to the point of obsession.

With her hand on the bedroom windowsill as a barre...Tashi was secretly doing some late-night ballet practice. Pliés *in first position, slow, back straight, the free arm sweeping down as the knees bent.*

She can't understand why her mum is so discouraging.

"*I won't ever be a ballerina. I know that,*" said Tashi. "*I'm not looking for flowers and fame and everything. I just...want to dance!*"

In Josephine Feeney's *Dancing Nancy*, Nancy longs to be like her cousin Geraldine, to wear black dancing shoes and a green dress with swirling patterns.

"*I want to go to Irish dancing classes!*" Nancy shouted. "*I want to learn how to dance!*"

But learning to dance isn't as easy as Nancy thinks. Not even Irish dancing, which looks so deceptively simple. Nancy soon learns that it's not just a question of hopping and skipping. She has a long way to go before she is ready to wear the green dress.

In *Jeffrey*, by Lynne Reid Banks, poor plump Janet doesn't want to learn ballet – *I was speechless, Me? Ballet? I actually managed to burst into tears.* But her mother has decided: what Janet needs is Advantages.

So I was bought a practice dress and ballet shoes... and when at last Madame had a vacancy, off I went, willy-nilly, to ballet class.

Where the star, without any doubt, is Jeffrey.

"*Fancy,*" sniffs Janet's nanny, "*a boy wanting to prance around doing ballet! Not very manly.*"

Every dance teacher dreams of having a student as gifted as Jeffrey. But this is the 1930s, and Jeffrey's dad doesn't think it right that a boy should dance...

As the person who compiled the collection, I have contributed two stories. One of them is *Curtain Call*, the tale of a dream come true. The other, *The Stuff that Dreams are Made Of*, is the tale of a dream which has to remain just that: a dream.

It is *my* story; my *own* story. Read it and you will understand why it is that I have made this collection!

Jean Ure
October, 1996

THE
STUFF THAT DREAMS
ARE MADE OF

Jean Ure

Ballet is the stuff that dreams are made of.

My particular dream started a long time ago. It started when I was ten years old and had pneumonia (which my mum always said I caught from walking round in bare feet and without my dressing gown, though I don't actually believe that you do "catch" pneumonia in this way).

Even after I had stopped having it and was well again, I was still rather pale and peaky and so the doctor said I must be sent away to a convalescent home, to recover my strength.

The convalescent home was at the seaside and perhaps I ought to have been excited, or at any rate grateful, because it wasn't every little girl who was lucky enough to go to the seaside in those bleak post-war days of the 1950s, but I was a bit of a wimp. I had never left my mum before and I spent the whole of the journey there in tears, and the whole of the first twenty-four hours weeping like a water spout.

And then came the day when the dream began.

I can remember it with far more clarity than I can remember the Coronation, which took place in that same year. In fact I can hardly remember the Coronation at all, for I don't think I was specially interested in it. But I can still see the big dining hall of the convalescent home, cleared of its tables and chairs, and us children – about a dozen in all, so my memory says, of assorted ages, between about six and eleven –

gathered in our shorts and aertex shirts at one end, while little Miss Pearce (short and dumpy) seated herself at the piano, and Miss Huxtable (tall, white-haired, imposing) clapped her hands for our attention.

"All right, children! Settle down! Today we're going to be butterflies…butterflies flitting from flower to flower. Light as feathers, floating in the air…Take a deep breath! Deep, deep…Fill your lungs. Can you feel yourselves getting lighter? So! When the music begins—"

I had never been a butterfly before. I had run and jumped and done handstands. I had played netball and rounders, and contorted my body into weird and wonderful shapes for the fun of it. But I had never been a butterfly!

I fluttered, I flitted, I was light as air. I made up little steps and let my arms fly up like thistledown. I forgot that I was homesick and that I wanted my mum. I was a butterfly, on wings of cobweb! Lost to the world, I flickered and floated.

And then the music stopped and I heard Miss Huxtable's voice: "Well! It seems we have a real little dancer in our midst."

The little dancer was me!

Every day for a fortnight I made up my own steps to the music that Miss Pearce played on the old upright piano. One day I was a willow tree, waving in the wind; the next I was a dolphin – or a cat – or a horse a-gallop over the plain.

I woke up every morning and no longer thought "I want my mum!" but "What will we be to the music today?"

I was glad to see my parents when they finally came to take me home. Of course I was! But at the same time I was desperately anxious to know that it wasn't going to be the end of my new-found delight in movement. I babbled and burbled about it all the way back to London on the train. "And then I was a butterfly, and then we had to be dolphins, and then I was a cat, moving ever so, e-v-e-r s-o delicately, like *this*."

My mum said, "I'm glad you enjoyed yourself, but we don't want to show off about it, do we?"

Showing off meant making a spectacle of yourself in public. Being noisy, rushing about. Making yourself *obvious*.

I wasn't being noisy or rushing about, but I suppose that slinking like a cat, ever so delicately, in a compartment full of people, could have been said to be making myself obvious.

So I obediently sat down again and continued my tale. "And then one day we had to be trees and I was a willow, *bending* in the breeze." And I bent from my sitting position and my hands crashed into the knees of the woman sitting opposite and my mum said, "Now that's enough! Just keep still."

"But I can have dancing lessons, Mum," I said, "can't I?"

"We'll see" said my mum.

"But I've got to!" I bawled, and my mum said, "Don't shout! I said we'll see."

For a whole year I nagged and pleaded with her. They had bought me a kitten as a coming-home present. He was called Bambi and was totally adorable. I loved him dearly, but if I had been given any choice in the matter I would have chosen to have dancing classes.

A few months later we got a dog, a wire-haired fox terrier called Buster. He was also adorable. Happy and sunny, though a bit of a punch-up merchant, and somewhat given to over-friendly greetings – my brother spent half his infancy wailing that "Buster bit my botty!" I loved Buster dearly, too. But I still would rather have had my ballet classes!

It had become almost a daily ritual.

"Mum, *please* let me learn ballet! Please, Mum! *Please!*"

The answer was always the same: "We'll see."

But time was passing and very soon I was eleven and was awarded a scholarship to the local posh school. This meant buying loads of posh uniform. Not just blouses and skirts, and blazers and sweaters, but white shorts for cricket and tennis, navy shorts for netball and gym, candy-striped dresses (in pink or blue or green) for summer, and long socks and short socks, and tennis shoes and hockey shoes, and even an extra special shoe bag to keep them in made out of "red Turkey twill". So now when I asked my pathetic question, the answer became: "We can't afford to throw away money on ballet lessons. We've got your school uniform to buy!"

My mum was a very straightforward, no-frills-no-nonsense kind of person. She genuinely didn't understand my terrible yearnings. And my dad was of the old school. He kept well out of it. Bringing up the children was women's business.

My gran came to live with us and what *she* said was that some people were simply never grateful. Thanks to my mum and dad making sacrifices when I was little (which they did), I was now privileged enough to be at one of the best schools in the country. What more did I want?

I wanted ballet lessons! Oh, I wanted them so badly!

"It's only a phase she's going through," said my gran. "She'll grow out of it."

But I didn't. If anything, I grew into it. I became obsessed, and spent every last penny of my pocket money feeding my obsession. I went to the ballet whenever I could. I bought ballet books. I bought tights and leotards and ballet shoes. My ballet shoes were the most precious objects I possessed! They were soft ones, of course. I knew I wasn't yet ready to go on point. I knew that I had a long way to go before my feet were strong enough for that. But I was working towards it! A pair of blocked shoes was my aim.

I practised in my bedroom, using the window sill as a *barre*. Every morning, every evening, copying the steps from a book called *Ballet for Beginners*, leaving the wardrobe door open so that I could see myself in the long mirror and check that my back was straight, that my bottom wasn't sticking out, that my ankles weren't rolling inwards. Positions of the feet, I mastered. Positions of the arms. *Pliés, battements, ronds de jambes, développés, arabesques, attitudes*...how I loved the sound of those words!

Centre practice was more difficult. Impossible, really, in a small suburban bedroom. Just one little *sauté* and I would be banging into the furniture. Anything more ambitious – a *grand jeté*, a *balloné*, a *pas de chat* – and Mum's voice would come shrieking up the stairs: "Stop that! You'll bring the ceiling down!"

My gran really hated me shutting myself away up there.

"What's she doing?" she used to say. "It's not natural! Why doesn't she get out and join the Girl Guides?"

She didn't know – nobody knew – that I was desperately attempting to make my dream come true.

On my way to school every morning I used to pass a ballet school – The Doran School of Dancing. A girl in my class went there. How I envied her!

How I longed to get there! I even sent away for a prospectus, which became almost as precious to me as my beautiful pink ballet shoes.

I used to watch this girl at school – Liz, her name was. I used to watch the way she walked, the way she stood, and try to copy her. She grew her hair long and wore it in a ponytail: I grew mine long and wore it the same way. I stood next to her in assembly and noted to my satisfaction that we were almost exactly the same height. When she came into school one day bringing her ballet shoes with her – *blocked* shoes – pink satin – I was so corroded with jealousy that I could hardly bear to look at her. (But secretly, inside myself, I was being her . . . I was Liz and the blocked shoes were mine!)

One day in gym the gym teacher said, "Did you notice who was the lightest on her feet?" And it was me! I was the one who was lightest on her feet! And I walked on air and hoped that Liz was looking at me and thinking, "That girl ought to be a dancer."

And maybe, just maybe, she would be so impressed that she would go to her teacher at the Doran and tell her about me . . .

But then another day a notice appeared on the notice board asking for "Anyone who learns ballet" to audition for the end-of-term show, and once again I was overwhelmed with jealousy. Even more so when the show went on and Liz not only danced in it but also did the choreography, and our English

22

teacher (whom I worshipped) singled her out for praise.

"Where is our budding choreographer? Blushing unseen in the back row? Show yourself and be congratulated!"

And all the class except me broke into loud hand-claps and I hated her. I *hated* her!

No, I didn't. It would be wrong to say that. I envied her, and I was fascinated by her. I wanted to be her!

I'd given up begging for ballet classes by now. I just knew that it wasn't going to happen, and in my heart of hearts, though I wouldn't have admitted it to myself, I knew that it was all too late. Fourteen I was, getting on for fifteen. Far, far too late. And yet I still kept up my daily practice. I still dreamed my secret dreams.

I almost thought, one summer, that they were going to come true after all. I enrolled for a three-day drama course, with money I had earnt from baby-sitting. The prospectus offered acting classes, speech classes, mime classes – and dancing!

The dancing was taken by a man who had been a minor soloist with Diaghilev. Rupert Doone, his name was. He was plump and bald and looked rather like an egg, but you could tell he had been a dancer from the way he moved. I was so eager to impress him! And I did – to begin with.

On the first day we did improvisation to music.

In the middle of the session Mr Doone came up to me and said, "You've obviously done a lot of ballet, haven't you?"

Why didn't I say no? Why didn't I tell him the truth, that I'd never had a ballet lesson in my life? I was too glowing with pride, that was why. An ex-soloist with Diaghilev had taken me – me! – for a trained dancer! It was almost my dream come true.

But pride, they say, precedes a fall. And when I fell, I fell hard.

Not on the second day. On the second day, we did "free movement". Mr Doone called us out in pairs. I was put with another girl, a girl called Verity.

"Now, I shall expect some real dancing from you two," he said.

Did he begin to suspect even then? No, I don't believe he did, for afterwards he nodded and said, "Thank you," in tones that were quite heartfelt, to both of us.

I suppose it was a bit of a come-down, for one who had danced with Diaghilev, to be conducting classes for a motley collection of wannabe theatricals. I daresay he was genuinely grateful to Verity and me.

But then, on the third day . . .

"*Pirouettes*," he said.

It was the *pirouettes* that were my downfall.

"*Pirouettes en dehors* . . . prepare in second. Weight evenly balanced. Right arm in front, left arm to the side. Open your right arm slightly and bring the left to meet it. Raise your working foot and turn sharply towards it. On to *demi-pointe*. So!"

It is not easy to teach yourself *pirouettes* in your bedroom. It is not easy to teach yourself *pirouettes* full stop. It is, in fact, well nigh impossible.

Just for starters, I had never even succeeded in mastering the technique of "spotting" – fixing your eyes to a certain point and whipping your head round faster than your body. It's that which enables a dancer to do *pirouette* after *pirouette* without getting dizzy. And I couldn't do it!

I couldn't even perform one pirouette with any sense of style.

Verity could. She had been learning ballet since she was a toddler. *Pirouettes* gave her no problems at all.

I could sense Mr Doone's puzzlement as I floundered and flobbed. I could sense the growing disillusion – I had let him down! He had been deceived. I was no more a dancer than the rest of them (apart from Verity). I could almost pinpoint the moment when disappointment turned to cold indifference.

If I had been writing a book, I would have made myself pretend a sudden injury – a dramatic fall to the floor clutching knee or ankle. Done anything to escape from my predicament. But somehow, in real life, you don't behave like that. In real life you soldier on, hoping against hope and all the evidence that things are not as dire as they seem.

But I knew that they were. I knew that I was thrashing about like a baby elephant caught in a trap.

At the end of class, rather curtly, as he took his leave, Mr Doone looked at me and said, "A pity! You could have made a dancer. Too late now, of course."

Just one more incident. When I was about sixteen or seventeen, a distant relative came to visit. She had never met me before.

"My goodness!" she remarked to my mother, "she walks just like a dancer."

"Funny you should say that," said my mother. "Do you remember" – she turned to me – "when you had pneumonia and went to that convalescent home? When we came to collect you, they told us then that we ought to let you have dancing classes. Perhaps we should have done! Who knows? You might have become a dancer."

When I went to drama school a year or two later, I met a girl who had danced with the Royal Ballet but had given it up. She told me that ballet was a mug's game.

"Half the people in it are neurotic, most of them are anorexic, and practically everybody's crippled by the time they're forty. It's just not worth it."

It might not have seemed worth it to her, but it did to me.

I'm grown up now, happily married and doing

my own thing, with a beloved family of rescued animals, but I still look back and wish with all my heart that I could have learnt ballet. Even today, when I see a young dancer clutching her pink satin ballet shoes, I feel pangs of envy. Especially if those shoes are blocked!

There are some dreams which just never leave you.

CLOSER THAN MOST
Sandy Asher

"Cathy! Amy! *Everybody*! Guess who's joining our class!"

I looked up from my dance bag to find Nina Sawyer and her twin sister Nikki all but toppling each other over as they burst into the dressing room.

"Betsy Murphy!" Nikki announced, before the rest of us could muster a guess. "She's due in here any minute now."

Maria Gomez nudged me with her elbow. "Cathy, who's Betsy Murphy?"

Maria had moved to Greenfield at the beginning of the school year, so she didn't yet know the local scene very well. She and I became fast friends the day she turned up at Greenfield Ballet. At thirteen we're the youngest dancers in the advanced class. The twins are next, at fourteen, and all the rest are fifteen and up.

While several girls gathered around the twins for further details, I quickly explained the situation to Maria. "Betsy Murphy is the only child of J.K. Murphy—"

"The rich guy?" Maria broke in.

"The *very* rich guy," I said. "He and his wife own half of Greenfield."

"More than half," Nina corrected me from across the room. She and Nikki are real sticklers for detail, especially when it comes to Greenfield Ballet gossip.

While wriggling into their tights and leotards, the twins gave Maria a full run-down of everything the Murphys owned: Murphy Towers, Murphy Industrial Park . . .

I watched and listened as I fixed my hair for class. Being shy myself, I love the twins' chatter. But in the mirror, I could see my sister Amy eyeing them with disapproval. She used to agree with me that the twins made the time before and after class almost as much fun as class itself. But now that she's a big-shot senior in high school, she fancies herself above all that.

"I thought Betsy Murphy was away at boarding school," she broke in suddenly.

"She *was*," Nina said. "She's been stashed away at boarding schools and summer camps for years. But she's back."

"Why?" I asked.

Nina and Nikki exchanged conspiratorial grins. "She hasn't been doing well at school lately," Nikki said. "Her parents want to keep a closer watch on her this year."

"How do you know all this stuff?" Maria asked.

Nina winked. "We stay alert."

"We stay twice as alert as most people," Nikki pointed out.

"Anyway," Nina went on, "Betsy's coming here to continue her dance training. Her mother's a big supporter of Greenfield Ballet, you know. She's president of the board of directors."

"What do you think she'll be like – this Betsy Murphy?" Maria asked.

"A total snob," Nikki predicted.

"But a very good dancer," Nina added.

Nikki agreed. "She's had the best training money can buy. Mrs Murphy always wanted to be a dancer, but *her* mom didn't approve, so she's dumped all her dreams—"

At that very moment, the dressing room door opened and Betsy Murphy walked in. I could hear breath being sucked in all around the room.

She was about my height, five foot two, with blonde hair pulled into a tidy bun above her lightly freckled face. She must have been Amy's age, fifteen, but she looked younger. Her pale blue eyes darted nervously around the room until Nikki piped up with a loud "Hi!" that made all of us jump and sent Betsy's gaze plummeting to the floor. And there it stayed, although she did manage a quiet "Hi" of her own.

Everyone stepped out of her way as she walked quickly to the far end of the room. There, with her back to us, she took off her coat and revealed a slender silhouette in black leotard and pink tights – the same uniform the rest of us wore. While we all stared wordlessly, Betsy drew a pair of ballet slippers out of a black canvas tote and put them on.

The awkward silence was fast becoming unbearable, but the pre-school class that met before ours was let out just then and tiny girls in bright leotards tumbled into the room.

"Time for class," Amy announced over their giggles, and I saw Betsy breathe a sigh of relief.

"Snob," Nikki whispered to me as we followed the others out the door.

But I knew shyness when I saw it.

Whatever classes Betsy had been doing poorly in at boarding school, ballet definitely was not one of them. From my first quick glances at her reflection in the studio mirror during *barre*, I could tell she had excellent technique. But she didn't seem to enjoy what she was doing – and anyone who didn't melt under the sunshine of Miss Laurie's smile was frozen solid indeed. The one place on earth I *never* felt shy was out on the floor, dancing for Miss Laurie.

"I believe," Amy had announced after our first class with her, "that we have met the most perfect person on earth."

I agreed. "The most perfect, the most beautiful, *and* the best dance teacher."

That was three years ago. Miss Laurie took over as Artistic Director of Greenfield Ballet when Miss Eva, our first teacher, retired. Miss Laurie insisted Amy and I both go into the advanced class – a terrifying move for eleven-year-old me at the time, but she convinced me I could do it. And I did.

Miss Laurie had risen to be a soloist with a professional company before an automobile accident damaged her right knee. Sometimes I thought I could detect a slight stiffness when she demonstrated a movement for us, but it could have been my imagination. The injury had left her a lovely dancer still, but one who would never again perform on stage.

If she was bitter about that loss, she never showed it. In fact, she seemed to love nothing more in the world than working with her "cygnets" as she called us. And there was nothing in the world we loved more than working with her.

Now, her radiant smile shone more often than not on Betsy Murphy, although it never did Betsy much good. She danced well, but her eyes remained downcast, and she spoke only when she couldn't avoid it.

Most of the time, the rest of us spared her the trouble, but her gloomy presence still managed to dampen our dressing room banter.

The volume didn't pick up again until auditions were announced for the annual *Nutcracker* ballet. Even if Betsy remained silent on the subject, we couldn't help but speculate on who would be chosen to dance which roles.

The Sugar Plum Fairy and her Prince would be guest artists, as usual, brought in from New York. But several of Greenfield Ballet's top dancers had gone away to college that autumn, which meant some of us coming up behind them might step into our first important solos. We'd been in the corps for the *Waltz of the Flowers* and *Snowflake Ballet*, but the lead roles of the Dewdrop Fairy and Snow Queen were dreams about to come true for two lucky dancers.

"Cathy's my choice for the Dewdrop Fairy," Nina decided, the day the audition notice went up.

Nikki nodded emphatically. "She's got the technique and the spirit."

I ducked my head to hide the blush creeping over my face – a blush of embarrassment *and* pleasure. I loved the *Waltz of the Flowers* and yearned to dance the Dewdrop Fairy.

But what were my chances? "Everyone in town gets to audition," I reminded the twins. "There'll be plenty of technique and spirit around."

"Mark my words," Nina insisted. "Miss Laurie has her eyes on you for a big solo, and you're not icy enough for the Snow Queen."

At that, half the heads in the dressing room turned towards Amy, and the other half sent Betsy Murphy diving into her dance bag for something she was obviously only pretending to need. *Her* blush, we soon discovered, was all embarrassment and no pleasure.

The twins were alone in the dressing room when Amy and I arrived the next Monday afternoon. They could hardly contain the latest news.

"Mrs Murphy was in Miss Laurie's office when we got here," Nina said.

"She was *shouting*," Nikki added. "We couldn't make out the words, but she left in a big huff."

Even Amy was intrigued by that. "Weird," she said.

And the weirdness continued. All week, there were phone calls before, during, and after class. Members of the Greenfield Ballet board of directors drifted in and out of Miss Laurie's office. Some huddled in the hallway, whispering; others watched our class, brows furrowed with concern.

Then Mrs Murphy showed up again, along with all the other board members, for a meeting that lasted well into our Friday afternoon class time.

We were all hanging around, not knowing what to think or do, when a board member suddenly called Betsy into the office. Several long moments later, the office door burst open and Betsy came hurtling out, eyes and nose flame-red from crying. "I'm sorry," she murmured to no one in particular as she ran into the dressing room and snatched up her dance bag and jacket. "It's not my fault. I'm *sorry*."

Before anyone could ask why, she and her mother were gone. The rest of the board members soon left as well. Then Miss Laurie called us into the studio for class and merely shook her head when Nina asked what had happened to Betsy.

At nine that Saturday morning, the *Nutcracker* auditions began in the Greenfield Civic Theater auditorium. When Amy and I arrived, some of the youngest dancers were already on stage, clustered around a tall man in black slacks and turtleneck sweater.

"Who's he?" I wondered aloud. "Where's Miss Laurie?"

"I don't know," Amy said. "But something's happened."

The blood chilled in my veins as we sped down the aisle and slid into the row behind the twins and Maria.

"What's going on?" Amy demanded.

The three of them turned to face us, eyes glistening with tears.

"Miss Laurie's been fired," Nina said.

"You're kidding!" I gasped.

"They've brought in the guy who's going to dance the Prince," Nikki informed us. "That's him up there. He flew in from New York last night."

"I just can't understand it," Maria whimpered. "How could they fire *Miss Laurie*?"

"I keep telling you," Nina said, "It's easy when you're on the board . . . and you donate tons of money."

"The Murphys?" Amy asked.

The twins nodded.

"But *why*?'

Nina took a deep breath, dabbed at her eyes with a tissue, and launched into the whole sad story. "Mrs Murphy thought it was all set up – when Betsy

enrolled, she would automatically dance the Snow Queen. But Miss Laurie insisted that Betsy audition like everyone else. So Mrs Murphy told the board she could no longer support the ballet if Miss Laurie stayed on as Artistic Director."

Amy slumped against the back of her seat. "That's disgusting!"

Maria turned to face her. "I think Miss Laurie was fighting for *you*, Amy."

"Well, I wouldn't do their *Nutcracker* now if the entire board came begging on their knees," Amy snapped.

The next thing I knew, she was dashing back up the aisle.

I charged after her. "Amy, wait! Where are you going?"

"Home."

"But what about the audition?"

"If Miss Laurie isn't going to be part of this, neither am I."

"*Amy!*" I tried to find a way to make her slow down, think it over, help *me* think it over, but the right words wouldn't come. She had a point. How could we go on dancing for a company that could treat Miss Laurie so unfairly?

But how could we *not* go on dancing?

Amy stopped for just a moment in the lobby. "Are you coming home with me or not?"

"I want to dance—" I began, weakly.

"Then dance," she said and shoved open the glass door. "But count me out of it!"

I dragged myself back down the aisle to where Maria and the twins sat swivelled in their seats, waiting for me.

"She's quitting," I informed them.

"I thought about it, too," Maria admitted.

"Sure, but what's the point?" Nina said. "They're not going to give Miss Laurie back her job just because a couple of dancers walk out. Look at this auditorium. There are plenty of dancers from other studios. I think we should stay here and win all the top roles. Show them Miss Laurie trained the best."

Just then, Betsy Murphy, being hurried along by her mother, brushed past us and took a seat in the first row.

"How could she bear to show up?" Maria whispered.

"Her mother wouldn't let her back out *now*, would she?" I asked. "I always knew Betsy was unhappy. Now I understand why."

"She did apologise," Maria remembered.

I nodded. "*She's* not the one who wanted things to turn out this way."

"Right," Nikki broke in. "So while she's dancing the Snow Queen and Amy's home with a broken heart, we'll all feel sorry for Betsy. Is that what you're saying?"

"I don't know what I'm saying," I admitted. But

I did feel sorry for Betsy. And Amy. And Miss Laurie. And all the rest of us.

The Prince's name was Carl Duvalle. Once he'd dismissed the littlest dancers, he became very businesslike and ran the audition the way I suppose a big-city audition would go. Groups were asked to learn combinations quickly, do them, and move on. One after another, dancers were sent from the stage with a polite, "Thank you very much." The auditorium seemed to grow larger and colder as more and more of them gathered their coats and bags and left.

Along with several dancers from other studios, those of us in Miss Laurie's advanced ballet class were told to stay, and stay and stay. We danced to the *Waltz of the Flowers*, the Spanish dance, the Russian, the Chinese . . . "Do it for Miss Laurie," Nina whispered, each time.

One by one, other dancers were sent home and we were left on stage, sweating, panting, and still fighting nerves and the knife-blade of sadness that came with each thought of Miss Laurie or Amy.

At last, there were no more "Thank you"s. "Very nice," Mr Duvalle told the few of us remaining. "We'll be in touch with you on Monday."

When I got home, I found Amy in her room, propped up in bed with a book she wasn't really reading.

"Do you want to know how it went?" I asked,

from her doorway.

"No," she said.

"Oh, come on, Amy! You're not going to stop dancing for ever—"

"Yes, I am."

"*Why?*"

"Because it's not perfect any more," she replied, as if that explained everything.

"What are you talking about?"

"Ballet has always been the one perfect thing in our lives – perfectly beautiful. Now it's all spoilt with board members, and money, and selfishness, and cruelty. I don't want to be part of it any more."

"I can't believe this," I told her.

"Believe it," she said.

And she meant it.

I had to admire the courage of her convictions. She made me feel ashamed for staying at the audition and for wanting to go on dancing, even with all the terrible things now attached to it. If I truly believed that what had happened to Miss Laurie was wrong, shouldn't I quit, too?

People quit all the time. When I was little, every girl I knew thought she was a ballerina – especially after we saw our first *Nutcracker*. Up and down the street we twirled, little paper tiaras in our hair. Then we discovered we'd actually have to *work* to become dancers, and, out of that group, only Amy and I enrolled in classes.

Every year since, dancers we knew found reasons to quit: cheerleading practice, boyfriends, college, job . . .

Now it was Amy's turn.

And mine?

All I'd ever wanted to do was dance. It had always been that simple! Not any more.

There was talk at dinner about Amy quitting, but nothing helpful. Mom and Dad weren't pleased, but they figured she might take it up again later. And anyway, college applications, exams, the prom, and graduation would be excitement enough for one year. As for me, to quit or not, they agreed, was a decision I had to make for myself.

Still unsure and deep in thought, I trudged down to the studio after school on Monday. Habit got me on and off the bus, across the familiar streets and up the stairs.

The pre-schoolers were just finishing up when I arrived, skipping in a happy circle around Mr Duvalle. Miss Laurie was alone in her office! For a moment, my heart soared. Then I realised she was wearing street clothes, not her leotard and tights. A cardboard box sat on the carpet near her desk. She was kneeling beside it, head bent over some papers.

"Hi, Miss Laurie," I said.

She looked up and smiled, but I could see weariness in her eyes. "Hello, Cathy. Hey – congratulations!"

She nodded towards a sheet of paper taped to the office door – the *Nutcracker* cast! I saw my name next to the words, Dewdrop Fairy. The thrill that ran through me was tinged with sadness, and more than a little fear. How could I take on a role like that without Miss Laurie? Tears choked my "Thank you".

Miss Laurie stood up, drew me into the office, and closed the door behind us. We sat facing each other on her old grey sofa.

"Amy says it's all spoilt," I managed to mutter. "And it used to be so perfect."

She listened quietly as I explained about Amy, then lifted my chin in her cupped hand and made me look her in the eye. "It was never perfect," she said. "Ballet is a striving *towards* perfection, but we're human, so we can never get there. Still, we dancers come closer than most. That's quite a privilege, isn't it? And it makes the striving a joy in itself."

"Then you're not going to quit ballet altogether?" I asked.

Miss Laurie laughed at the idea. "I didn't quit when I hurt my knee, and I'm certainly not going to quit now. Artistic Directors and board members are always locking horns over one thing or another. I'm not the first to lose a job over it."

"I wish there were no board of directors," I said.

"Then there'd be no studio, no *Nutcracker*," she reminded me. "They're the ones who raise the money, so we can be the ones who dance. In spite of the disagreements, we need them."

I sighed, agreeing reluctantly. "Where will you go?" I asked her.

"I'll find something – perhaps with a company you'll want to join someday."

I couldn't help grinning at that. "They'll be lucky, whoever gets you," I said.

"Thank you, Cathy. The same goes for you. Because you're not going to quit either, are you?"

I shook my head, and her smile bathed me in its old radiance.

"I'm sorry Amy's given up," she said softly, "but it's easy to love something you believe is perfect. The challenge is to go on loving even when you realise it's not. That's the test of a real dancer."

She stood up then and walked towards the door – and I definitely saw the stiffness in her knee. That's when I knew Miss Laurie would always be with me, wherever and whenever I danced. Perfection was a dream, but we'd already come closer than most.

OLÉ!

Adèle Geras

Mrs Goodbody (known as 'Goody Twoshoes') pushed her glasses as far up her nose as they would go, opened her mouth, and spoke in her you'd-better-listen-to-this-it's-very-important voice:

"*What's in a name? that which we call a rose*
By any other name would smell as sweet.

"That's what Juliet says in the play, children, as you know. What did Shakespeare mean by it, and do we agree?"

Dympna began to doodle in her rough book. She wasn't going to say so in class and get laughed at, but she seriously thought she'd never heard so much rubbish in her whole life, and she didn't care if it *was* by Shakespeare. Her own name had caused her nothing but pain, misery and heartache. Dympna. It was a name that sat up and begged to be altered into something ridiculous: Dimps, Dimples (her grandmother's favourite) and now, worst of all, Dumpy. It seemed to her that almost before she had come in through the gates of Forest Hills High School in September, there was a group of giggling, extremely skinny girls in black tights ready to stick the nickname on her as she made her way to her first assembly.

"Don't take any notice of them," said Ruth, who had been her best friend all through primary school and who, thank goodness, was going to be in the same class. "They look like spiders."

"It's easy for you to say," Dympna answered. "There's not much anyone can do with a name like Ruth."

"The main thing," said Ruth, being sensible as usual, "is that whatever they call you, you are not dumpy."

That may have been true then, Dympna thought, but she wasn't altogether sure it still was. She squirmed in her seat. If her name had been something long and slim like Melissa or Alexandra, maybe her body would have grown long and slim to match. Having "Dumpy" flung at you by all and sundry was probably guaranteed to stunt your growth and thicken your ankles. Dympna remembered another conversation she'd had with Ruth:

"It's extremely dumpy-ist," Ruth said, "to object to being called Dumpy. Who says everyone has to be as tall and thin as a telegraph pole?"

Dympna sighed. Ruth had never understood about ballet.

"Being dumpy *doesn't* matter in real life," she explained. "It only matters in ballet. In ballet, your body has to be perfect."

Ruth snorted. "Perfect according to ballet standards. I don't think much of them. They look like stick insects to me."

Dympna giggled. "I suppose some of them do,"

she admitted "but they have to be light for their partners to pick them up. I used to be all right. It's only lately that I've become . . . well . . . dumpy."

Goody Twoshoes's voice broke into Dympna's thoughts.

"I'd like you all to write an essay about it, please. At least four sides of paper and give it some serious thought."

"What's the essay supposed to be about?" Dympna whispered to Ravina, who sat next to her. Ruth had long ago been moved to the other side of the classroom, in what Goody called "a last-ditch stand to put a curb on your incessant chattering."

"Weren't you listening?" Ravina whispered. "It's about that rose stuff . . . about names. We have to discuss it and say if we agree or not."

"Right," said Dympna. "I know what I think about that. I can easily write four sides."

Galina, Larissa, Natalia . . . those were good ballet names. Dympna turned them over in her mind as she walked home. Viviana was fine, like Viviana Durante, but Darcey Bussell must have had to be extra good all her life to get over her surname. Well, she was. All sorts of ballet dancers changed their names, and Dympna had seriously considered doing this herself for a while. In fact, it had been a possibility until last week, when suddenly the dreadful truth had glared at her in the changing room: she would never make a ballet dancer. She'd been standing in her pink leotard, next to Natasha (very ballet-ish name!), and just happened to glance across at the mirror. Natasha looked fragile, brittle, almost transparent. She looked as if a sigh from someone standing next to her would blow her across the room, whereas Dympna looked . . . well, she looked solid. She looked healthy. She had thighs and hips and cheeks and, horror of horrors, a bust that seemed to be getting bigger every time she caught sight of it. She did not look dumpy, though. Her legs were too long for that, but she would never be a ballet dancer, not by any stretch of the imagination.

That night, at supper, Dympna made her announcement.

"It's the last lesson before half-term next week," she said, "and then I'm not going to ballet ever again."

Her mother paused with a fork halfway to her mouth.

Her father swallowed a Brussels sprout and started coughing.

Her little sister, Dulcie, said, "Why on earth? I can't believe it! You've always been mad about ballet. What happened?"

Dympna looked round at her family. Her mother's mouth hung open. Her father's eyes were still streaming.

"I'm the wrong shape," she said.

"Did Miss Elena say so?" Dulcie asked.

"No, but she never chooses me for any special things. I wasn't even one of the mice in the *Nutcracker* at Christmas, and almost everyone else was."

"Does that matter?" asked Dad. "If you enjoy it, does it matter that you can't be the best? You don't have to make a career of it, you know. You could do it just for fun. For exercise." Dympna rolled her eyes up to the ceiling and groaned. If she'd explained it once, she'd done so a hundred times.

"Ballet," she said, "isn't for fun. It isn't for exercise. I could take Bobs for a walk if I wanted to do exercise. Or go swimming. Ballet is a way of life. Ballet is a state of mind. Ballet is a religion."

She was quoting Miss Elena, but it sounded impressive, and, sure enough, her parents couldn't think of a word to say. Dympna helped herself to another spoonful of buttery mashed potatoes, thinking: it doesn't matter now. Not if I'm never going to dance again. She started to eat, but suddenly felt so overcome with misery that the food tasted like mud in her mouth.

"I've got to do my homework now," she said, pushing her chair back and standing up. "I've got an essay to write."

* * *

Upstairs in her bedroom, Dympna took her special

53

ballet suitcase out of the cupboard and put it on the bed. Four years ago, when it had been her main birthday present, she'd thought it was the most beautiful object in the whole world. Now, the gold paint had flaked off the picture of the ballerina painted on the lid, and the pink had turned pale grey from being thrown around the changing room each week. Dympna opened the case and spread everything out all over the duvet – the leotard, the cardigan that fastened at the back, the pins and hairnet, the white tights, and the two pairs of ballet shoes. There was something terribly sad, Dympna thought, about ballet shoes when no one was wearing them. "I shan't get rid of these," she said to herself. "I'll give the rest of the stuff to Oxfam, but not these. I'll hang these up somewhere so I can look at them, and remember how I loved them; loved putting them on and tying the satin ribbons in exactly the right way; loved the way my feet felt in them . . . dainty, pointed, beautiful . . . loved the feeling they gave me that I could dance and dance forever until there was no more music left in the whole world." Dympna walked over to her dressing table and sat down and stared into the mirror.

"I'll never dance again," she said aloud, and noticed that her eyes had filled with tears and that a couple of them had actually begun to slide down her cheeks.

Dympna had always thought of herself as someone

who had no trouble at all giving things up. Every Lent, she went without something (sweets or biscuits or cups of hot chocolate last thing at night), and after the first day or two she hardly missed whatever it was she'd decided to sacrifice. Giving up ballet seemed to be different, and much harder. Dympna found herself doing things like holding on to the towel rail in the bathroom and going through some of her *barre* exercises. And she could not escape music. It didn't have to be ballet music. Every single thing she heard when she turned on her radio made Dympna want to move. She found herself doing solitary tap routines, or lonely waltzes, or even some of the baby stuff they used to do in primary school Music and Movement – like being a tree swaying in the wind, or a wave breaking on the shore. My arms need to stretch themselves, she thought. My feet want to dance, but none of these modern things makes me as happy as ballet did.

She glanced at the pink satin ballet shoes still waiting on her bookshelf to be put up in an artistic display of some kind. Maybe, Dympna thought, they were like the Red Shoes in the story that made it impossible for Karen to stop dancing, only even more magical. Perhaps they had passed on a kind of ballet addiction which didn't leave her when she took them off, and which seemed to have spoilt her taste for any other kind of dancing.

Dympna and Ruth were in Ruth's bedroom cutting pictures from a pile of magazines for an Art project. They were supposed to stick all sorts of images together to make a collage.

"This is what we used to do in primary school," said Dympna. "I'm sure we're meant to be doing harder stuff now. I thought Art was going to be drawing and painting and things."

"Mr Dewar says putting the right images together *is* like painting. In a way. You have to choose things that look good next to one another."

"Seems too easy to me," said Dympna, snipping away, "but it's good fun, too. Pass me that one over there."

Ruth gave Dympna the magazine, and went on with her own snipping. Dympna turned the pages. Then she stopped.

"Look at this," she said. "Isn't it lovely?"

Ruth looked. "It's just a sherry advertisement. Those are called flamingo dancers. Or something."

Dympna laughed. "Flamenco dancers, silly. Not flamingo. It's a special kind of dancing, that the Spanish do. I've read about it."

"With castanets?"

Dympna nodded. She was still gazing at the picture, which showed six dancers, twisting to the music of a guitar, with their arms held high above their heads.

"Can I cut it out and keep it?" she asked Ruth.

"Don't see why not,' said Ruth, "but I can't see why you like it so much."

Dympna put the picture in her Geography file to keep it flat. She didn't know why it appealed to her. She only knew that she wanted to look and look at it, so hard that she could almost pretend she'd walked into it.

That evening, Dympna stuck the picture to the inside of her cupboard, next to her special ballet postcards. How lovely the ruffled skirts were! So many flounces and frills! There was a woman in a dress that looked just like one of those white carnations whose petals are edged in scarlet. Another woman wore yellow, and in the background you could just see a man in black playing a guitar. The more she stared at the photograph, the more Dympna's eyes were drawn to a figure in the bottom right-hand corner of the page. You could only see part of her: her arms, half her face and half her body, down to just below her waist; but even part of her was enough. Dympna stared again. It was true. This woman was old. She must have been at least fifty. There was grey in her hair. There were little wrinkles round her eyes and at the corners of her mouth. She was looking down, at her feet perhaps, and that gave her a double chin. She had a bosom. Not an enormous one. Not what Ruth called "a balcony", but a bosom nevertheless. Her dress was shiny, electric blue with black ruffles all round the plunging neckline. Dympna couldn't take her eyes off the picture. There was no getting away from it. This woman was old! She was plump. She was quite possibly dumpy, and yet she was beautiful, and more amazing even than that, she was DANCING! Dympna closed her cupboard door. She sat down at the dressing table, raised her arms above her head and clicked her fingers. She didn't know much about flamenco dancing, and even less about Spain, but she *did* know one thing:

"Olé!" she said to her reflection, and she liked the sound of it so much that she said it again. "Olé!"

Over the next few days, Dympna found herself drumming her heels on every bit of wooden floor she happened to walk on, and practising her finger-clicking until all her friends begged her to stop.

One day, she discovered a long red skirt lurking at the bottom of Dulcie's dressing-up box. It actually had a frill around the hem, and Dympna raced back to her room to try it on. She changed quickly into her black school leotard, and then pulled on the skirt. She couldn't think of a way to do ruffles on the bodice, but she tied her best red scarf around her neck and scraped her hair back away from her face, just as she used to do for ballet class. Then she looked again at the sherry advertisement. *This* was the way the arms went . . . and the head was tilted like this . . . no, more like this. Dympna turned on the radio. The music that poured out had a driving, jazzy rhythm. It wasn't flamenco. Dympna knew that, but there was a guitar playing. The beat was insistent. It crept into her body from her arms (high above her head now, just like the dancers in the picture) and tingled its way down through her body until it reached her feet. She knew it was pointless to try and drum her heels on the carpet, but she couldn't stop herself. On and on she went, clicking her fingers in time to the rhythm, and twirling in front of the mirror. She caught a glimpse of herself as she spun round, and she looked . . . Dympna couldn't find a word to describe how she looked. Nor how she felt. Alive. She felt alive. She felt on fire. She felt breathless. When the music changed to a tinkly tune on strings, she sank to the floor, exhausted. I want to dance like that again, she thought, only properly this time. I want to look and see how they do it, and then I want to do it too. I know I do. I must. I absolutely must.

It had been Ruth's brilliant idea to ask Mr Baldwin, the Spanish teacher, for a video.

"Flamenco?" said Mr Baldwin, stroking his little beard. "Fascinating . . . fascinating . . . gypsy music, you know. Full of Arabic influences, of course . . . very wild and passionate stuff . . . very stirring. I don't know that I've got all that much. There's probably a bit on my *Look at Spain* tape. I can't let you take it home, I'm afraid, but you're welcome to come and look at it in the dinner hour. I'll be up in the Modern Language block today. I'll run it for you."

"Thank you, sir," said Dympna, and wondered how she could make the morning go faster. In three hours, she was going to see some real flamenco dancing . . . only three hours to wait.

The video had been a great disappointment.

"I'm sorry," said Mr Baldwin. "There wasn't very much of it, was there?" Dympna shook her head.

"What you need to do," he continued, "is to go to the Central Library. Go to the Music Section. I'm sure they'll have CDs and tapes, and possibly even a video."

"Yes, sir," said Dympna. "I will, sir. And thanks very much for showing me the video."

All through the rest of the afternoon, Dympna replayed, in her head, the two and a half minutes of dancing she'd seen on Mr Baldwin's tape. She had watched it three times. Now, there was a teacher standing in front of the class talking to them about something, but Dympna was miles away. Today was Friday. She would take the bus to town tomorrow morning and look for music and videos in the library. But she knew that wasn't going to be enough. She wanted to dance like that herself. She wrote the words in her rough book, in capital letters:

I WANT TO BE A FLAMENCO DANCER

and spent the rest of the lesson decorating the sentence with little doodles of flowers and guitars and hands holding what she hoped looked like castanets.

On Saturday morning, at the exact time she should have been at the library, Dympna was sitting next to Dulcie in the back of the car on the motorway. She was grumbling, even though she knew it was her own fault that in her fever of excitement over flamenco dancing she had completely forgotten about Aunty Mona's wedding anniversary.

"You could have left me behind," she said. "I could have spent the night with Ruth. I don't even like Aunty Mona much, and as for Uncle Gerald…"

Dympna's mother said, "I expect you'll stop grumbling when you see the food. You usually do. Mona says it's a lovely restaurant. She says there's live music. That'll be nice, won't it?" Dympna snorted. She imagined ladies in black dresses playing squeakily on violins, and cheered herself up by thinking ahead to next Saturday, when she would take the bus to town, and begin her research.

Dympna wasn't eating. She felt as though she had been holding her breath for hours; as though her whole body was filled with electricity, just waiting to fizz out all over the restaurant. Aunty Mona hadn't mentioned the most important thing about this place – it was SPANISH! The food was Spanish, the wine was Spanish, the name of the restaurant, *Casa Tapas*, was Spanish, and soon, soon there would be Spanish Dancing. It said so in big letters on the blackboard above the bar: *Mercedes y Jaime: Flamenco Dancers. Saturday and Sunday only*. Dympna looked at Aunty Mona and Uncle Gerald with new affection. How kind of them to invite the whole family from the other side of the country to share in the celebration of their wedding anniversary! How clever of them to know exactly what Dympna wanted most in the world!

But where were they? Mercedes and Jaime were nowhere to be seen.

"They'll be along soon," said Mum. "Don't fret. Have some salad."

"It's OK," said Dympna. "I'm not hungry."

"Are you sickening for something?" said Dad. Dympna shook her head. How could she explain that she felt nearly sick with longing and anxiety?

What if Mercedes had sprained her ankle on the way to the restaurant? Dympna was imagining a waiter making an announcement any minute now. . . But what was that? Castanets! Oh, yes, castanets . . . the unmistakable sound of wood on wood, and the vibrations of the guitar. They were coming. So far, only waiters had gone in and out of the door at the back of the restaurant. Now, it swung open and a young woman in a scarlet dress clicked out in high-heeled shoes. She took up a position not two feet away from Dympna. Behind her, a tall young man with hair like patent leather, and long legs in black trousers, began to drum his heels on the floor. No one spoke. Everyone stopped eating and stared. Dympna felt herself taking in every step of the dance, absorbing it, concentrating on it, making sure that she would always, *always* remember it. How beautiful Mercedes was! No one could call her skinny, her arms and shoulders were plump and curved, and her skin was like cream velvet.

When the dance ended, everyone clapped, except for Dympna. She stood up and ran to the door through which Mercedes and Jamie were disappearing. She called after them, "Please, Mercedes . . . *por favor* . . . may I speak to you? Umm . . . *es posible hablar con Usted*?"

Mercedes laughed. "Listen to this, Jaime! Someone thinks I'm Spanish!"

Dympna blushed. "I'm sorry. You must think I'm mad, only I've never seen flamenco dancing before and it's so lovely and I want to do it and I don't know how to begin, and—" Dympna's voice faded away as she began to realise she was doing what Ruth called "wittering on".

"We do not have a dressing room," said Jaime, "but we will come to your table to talk, if you wish."

Dympna ran back to the table and explained everything.

"Jaime is Spanish," said Dympna. "You can tell from his accent. Is it all right if they come and sit down for a moment?"

"We'd be honoured," said Uncle Gerald. "They can have a drink with us."

Dympna followed the others to the car park. It was late. Mercedes and Jaime had sat at the table and let Dympna ask them everything she could think of about flamenco dancing. The biggest surprise of the evening came when Mercedes told everyone where she had trained. It wasn't in Seville. It wasn't in Cordoba. It wasn't in Malaga. It wasn't even in Spain, but in Britain, and not just in Britain, but in Manchester, not more than a twenty-minute bus ride away from Dympna's own front door!

Uncle Gerald had torn a page out of his notebook for Mercedes to write down the name and telephone number of the teacher: Pilar de las Flores: 0161-564-5687. What a wonderfully kind man he was! Why had she not noticed this before?

Dympna danced all the way to where the car was parked.

She drummed her heels on the pavement, stamped her feet, and tossed her arms in the air.

"Stop it!" Dulcie whispered. "People are staring at us. They think you're daft."

Dympna smiled at Dulcie, and at a woman who just happened to be getting into her car, a few feet away.

"I don't care," she told them both. "I'm a flamenco dancer. Olé!"

THE GHOST
OF A CHANCE
Jean Richardson

The diary was one of Gran's special – Sophie called them weird – presents.

Her younger sister Charlotte, known as Charley, thought Gran gave the best presents in the world, but Sophie hated them.

"They're always old things," she said. "Things other people have used. I'm sure she buys them at car boot sales or from those smelly charity shops."

"She can't afford new things," Charley said defensively. "And she doesn't understand things like video games or CD-ROMs. Gran says her presents are for the imagination."

"Like that smelly old dress she gave you."

"It wasn't smelly. Well a bit, but it was quite a clean smell. Mum said it had probably been hanging in a wardrobe with lots of mothballs."

The diary had an odd smell too, sort of musty. It was satisfyingly fat, with a dark green leather cover that had no lettering on it, so that at first Charley didn't realise what it was. What she loved was the brass clasp that held the gold-edged pages tight shut. It fastened with a tiny lock to which, miraculously, the key had survived.

"How like Gran to give you a diary halfway through the year," said Sophie, who was secretly rather envious. "What year's it for? I bet it's not this year. Someone's probably written in it, too."

"It doesn't seem to be for any year," said Charley, "and no one's written in it. The pages tell you the date, not the day of the week, so you can start anywhere." She looked at Gran's card. "Gran says it's to record the most important year of my life."

"Big deal," sniffed Sophie, but Charley knew what Gran meant. Gran understood how Charley felt about dancing, knew that somehow this year she had to arrange full-time training. I'll write it all down, Charley told herself, and then when I'm a famous dancer, I'll be able to look back and see how I did it.

Sophie had gone to dancing classes too, until she'd decided they were boring. But dancing wasn't a passing craze for Charley. Right from the beginning, when it wasn't much more than running around to music, she'd found it magical. It made sense to her feet. She'd only have to watch steps once, and she would remember them and see how they fitted the music. Although she'd have felt shy about acting or singing in front of an audience, dancing came naturally.

Gran understood because she'd wanted to dance herself. "Perhaps you get it from me," she told Charley. "I was all for seeing myself as Margot Fonteyn, but it didn't work out."

"Why?" Charley liked having Gran to herself.

"I suppose I wasn't good enough. You need to

go to a special school to be really good, and there wasn't the money for that. When I was your age, it was just after the war and there wasn't lots of ballet like there is today. I only saw one ballet, and that was a very special treat."

"What was it?"

"*The Sleeping Beauty*. It wasn't the Royal Ballet in those days. They were called the Sadlers Wells Ballet, because they used to dance at the old Sadlers Wells theatre in Islington. They were very good, especially ballerinas like Margot Fonteyn and Moira Shearer."

"I've seen Shearer. She was in that film *The Red Shoes*, wasn't she? I got Dad to video it because it was about ballet. Did you mind not being a dancer, Gran?"

"I was a bit disappointed at the time, but I don't think the world lost a Fonteyn. I got interested in other things. It's the people for whom there aren't any other things who make it."

"There aren't other things for *me*," Charley said firmly. "Perhaps that means I'm going to make it."

But Gran was right about going to a special school. Charley knew all about them. They cost thousands of pounds a term. If Charley was going to get there, she'd have to get a grant or a scholarship, which meant she'd have to be *very* special. Not just the most special dancer at the Pavlova School, but better than the most special dancers from dozens of similar small schools. They all had girls as good as Charley.

She was thinking about this when she wrote her first entry in the diary.

2 May

Showed Mum and Dad the prospectuses Gran had sent for. Dad hit the roof when he saw how much it would cost. Dancing is fine for fun, he said. Just keep it that way. Mum was kinder but not really encouraging. They don't understand that
I HAVE TO DANCE.

When she'd finished, Charley locked the diary and put it back in her chest of drawers. She didn't trust Sophie not to read it, so she put the little key on her charm bracelet. This was another present from Gran that was much scorned by Sophie.

But longing to dance and being good at it weren't always the same thing. Nothing went right at Charley's next class. Her arms and legs refused to obey her, so that she felt clumsy and out of step with herself. She was near to tears by the end of class and couldn't bear to walk home with her best friend Sam, who'd done everything right.

She was grumpy all through tea even though it was her favourite pizza. She left the table as soon as she could and went to her bedroom. She felt angry – and scared. What if she *wasn't* good enough? Perhaps I'll feel better, she thought, if I write something down.

She unlocked the diary and flipped through the pages, looking for the one entry she'd made so far. There was some writing on a page in May, but to her surprise it was small and in green ink. Sophie was right after all, she thought, someone else *had* written in the diary, but where was her entry? All the other pages seemed to be blank. Puzzled, she turned back to the green writing.

2 May

What's the matter with me? I used to be so good at exercises, but today Miss Middleton made an example of me. Not what Mr H. would have expected of his prize pupil, she said. The old cat! She's just jealous because Mr H. went out of his way to talk to me at the last show. He believes in me. Thinks I ought to go to the SW school.

Charley read the entry several times. It was frustrating not to know who'd written it, or what the writer – who sounded like a she – was talking about. Who was Mr H., and what was the SW school? It's odd, she thought, but I could have written the first two lines. It sounds just like me.

Somehow, she didn't feel angry any more, and was able to step back and look at herself from the outside.

21 May

Class was awful, I was awful. I was trying too hard. Once something goes wrong, I don't seem able to put it right. I'm so dependent on being praised. When Mrs P. says "Well done," I feel really good, but when she doesn't say anything, I just know nothing will come right. I must try and remember what fun dancing used to be.

This time Charley hid the diary under a pile of knickers. The green writing wasn't at all like Sophie's, but it was the sort of trick she'd love to play. Charley wondered what had become of her entry. Perhaps Sophie had got hold of some super Tippex that left the page like new.

There was nothing worth recording the next day, but she unlocked the diary to see if anything had happened. The green entry was still there, and so was the one she'd written last night. Perhaps Sophie hadn't had time to remove it, or she couldn't find the key.

She'd shown Gran's prospectuses to Mrs P., who'd arranged a meeting with Mum and Dad. Sam's parents had already entered Sam for several auditions, but Sam was their only child and her mother was mad about ballet.

After the meeting, Charley had something really special to record in her diary, but she couldn't slip away to her room because it was be-extra-nice-to-Mum-and-Dad time. It was bedtime before she could unlock the diary. The entry for 21 May was now in green writing.

21 May

The SW Ballet are coming. I may be able to dance

in "The Sleeping Beauty"! They need peasant girls,
knitting women and mice. Hope I don't have to be
a mouse, as they don't do any dancing. Gillian's
aunt, who knows the ballet mistress, is going to
make sure she's a peasant. I hate Gillian. Wish my
aunt had a few ballet connections, but no such luck.

SW must stand for Sadlers Wells, and could it be the same *Sleeping Beauty* that Gran had seen? But that was about fifty years ago. The diary certainly looked old, but was it that old, and who'd written in it? Someone very like Charley from the sound of her. There must be lots of old diaries around, she thought, kept by people to remind them of their younger selves, just as she was planning to keep hers. What was really weird about this one, though, was that it seemed to be blank – until Charley wrote in it.

She had to concentrate to write down her own news.

9 June

Mum and Dad talked to Mrs P. about what I should do. She explained that I wouldn't get a grant unless I got into the Royal Ballet Lower School, which is like getting into heaven. But some of the other schools have scholarships, and there's a second chance to try for the RB school at sixteen. Dad asked if I was in with a chance, and Mrs P. said, "It's very difficult to tell at her age. She's keen, she moves well and is quick to learn. She's got good feet, and a nice sense of music. I think

*she should go for it and try not to be too
disappointed if it doesn't come off." So that's what
we agreed. I'm to audition for the Royal Ballet
School and several other schools. I'm so excited I
can't sleep. I'll never ask God for anything else if
only I can make it.*

It was the longest entry so far, and ran over on
to the next page. It would take a lot of Tippex to
paint out.

But the next time Charley got out the diary, her
entry had been replaced by no less than three green
ones. The ghostly dancer was over the moon about
The Sleeping Beauty.

9 June

*I'm a peasant girl and we have to do some peasant
dances and several grandes promenades. I'm going
to dance on the same stage as Margot Fonteyn!!
Some of the older girls are auditioning for the SW
school. They give themselves awful airs and keep
trying to chat up members of the company,
especially the boys.*

12 June

*Princess Aurora was superb, especially in the Rose
Adagio. We all held our breath when she stood on
point – but she didn't even wobble. I'd die to be
able to dance like Fonteyn. She's pure magic.*

21 June

*Tonight was the final performance. Everyone was
very tearful. The audience clapped and cheered and*

kept calling Fonteyn back to take another bow.
Joan and I hung round the stage door hoping to see
her. When she finally came out, carrying a vast
bouquet, she gave us the most lovely smile. We
danced all the way home.

A strange shiver – and it wasn't cold – ran through Charley. Sophie didn't know a thing about ballet, so she couldn't possibly have written that. But who had? Gran? But the writing wasn't at all like Gran's and, besides, Gran had never danced in a real ballet. Could it have been someone who might have been a famous dancer if . . . if something hadn't happened to her. An accident perhaps, or maybe she'd died.

Charley thought of asking Gran where she'd found the diary, but Gran liked being mysterious. "I have my sources," she'd say, which could mean anything. Sophie was probably right about Oxfam or a car boot sale, and no one knew where those things came from.

I'm going to LONDON! read the entry for 27 July.
To audition for the SW school, which really is the
only school to go to. If I get a place, it will mean
they think I've got talent – and if I don't . . . then
I'm not meant to be a dancer. But first, I'm to have
lessons with someone who used to dance with the
Diaghilev company. It will be like touching history.
I'll be dancing with someone who danced with
Nijinksy and Karsavina!

Charley wasn't sure who Nijinsky and Karsavina were, so she looked them up in a ballet dictionary. They turned out to be Russian dancers who'd come to the West after the Revolution. Nijinsky was said to be the greatest male dancer of all time.

She'd begun to feel a strong kinship with the unknown dancer. It was like having a secret best friend who wanted the same things but wasn't a rival like Sam. Perhaps the connection between them was that they were both auditioning for the same school, and cared so passionately about dancing that they were drawn to each other across the years.

Writing in the diary was like talking to a friend, a friend who could be trusted and who understood as no one else did. Charley started to write up her diary every day. The entries got longer and longer as she put down what happened at school and in dance class, and all her hopes and fears. It didn't matter that what she wrote had disappeared the next time she opened the diary. She felt sure that her words still existed somewhere, and would one day reappear as mysteriously as the green entries had done.

And then things began to go wrong. There was a series of green entries about living in London, feeling homesick, and having to fit in ordinary lessons with coaching from the Russian.

10 September

What an extraordinary man my Russian is. He darts round the studio and suddenly flies through the air. It's such an honour to be partnered by him, but oh, I wish my feet didn't hurt so. I daren't tell anyone, but some days they're so painful after class that I can hardly walk. I've tried soaking them in hot water, a bandage, plasters, resting whenever I can, but point work is agony. There's no such thing as a ballerina who can't stand on point. I ought to stop dancing for a couple of weeks, but I can't with the audition coming up.

4 October

My feet are worse. I had to stop dancing today because they hurt so. Monsieur was very kind but he insists that I see a doctor.

Charley had been practising so much that she'd developed a couple of blisters and was worried that they might not heal in time for *her* auditions. Mrs P. kept assuring her that they weren't looking for a display of virtuoso technique but an idea of how she moved and her line and musicality. "I've known the most unlikely girls get chosen," she said, "because of some innate quality, some potential that only a trained eye can see. Just try and relax and look as though you're enjoying yourself."

Fat chance of that, Charley thought.

She'd begun to feel that her success was in some way bound up with that of her ghostly partner.

Her problem sounded more serious than a couple of blisters, but they both shared a determination to dance whatever the cost. She had helped Charley to see how important it was to be determined. She was dedicated in a way that even Sam wasn't.

7 October

The doctor referred me to the hospital. I didn't like the consultant much. He wasn't at all sympathetic. Sent me off to be X-rayed. I have to go back next week.

She would be going to the doctor on the same day as Charley's first audition. Was it some kind of omen?

14 October

It was easier than I thought, Charley wrote that night. *We did some exercises at the bar, pliés and such like, and then some work in the middle. The teacher showed us a simple enchainement which we had to memorise and then do one at a time. The principal and three teachers watched us, and wrote their comments down on clipboards. The worse thing was having to stand around while they looked at us. Their expressions didn't give anything away. Mrs P. wasn't allowed to watch and was horribly jolly afterwards.*

The next night, Charley turned quickly to her last entry. As usual it had vanished, and in its place was a green entry. The writing was agitated and smudged, as though something wet, a tear perhaps, had splashed it. Charley knew at once it was not good news.

14 October

It's all over. All my dreams. I'll never be a dancer. I've thought of nothing else for years, practised for hundreds of hours, and yet in just a few minutes a man who knows nothing about me has put an end to everything. "I advise you to give up dancing," he said after looking at my X-rays. "There's nothing wrong with your feet for ordinary purposes, but if you persist in dancing, you'll do serious damage." Apparently ballet dancers need first and second toes of the same length. Because my big toe is longer, when I stand on point my whole weight rests on just one toe. I thought I was meant to be a dancer. I've shut everything else out of my life, and now my feet say no. It's all been for nothing.

Charley locked the diary and pushed it into the bottom drawer, burying it like a frightened animal under a pile of sweaters. Ever since she'd started writing in the diary, she and her ghostly partner had been dancing together. Now, one or perhaps both of them had come to a full stop. Charley couldn't bear to think that what they might have in common was not success but failure.

It was some weeks later, after she'd been offered a place at a Royal Ballet School summer course and a scholarship at another school, that Charley felt she could face the diary again. Now that she was on top of the world, she longed to be able to comfort the friend for whom it had gone so terribly wrong. Perhaps, she thought, if I write something down, the message will somehow get through to her.

But when she retrieved the diary and unlocked it, she saw at once that it looked different.

There were no entries at all in green ink. Just pages and pages in Charley's writing. It was, as Gran had forecast, a record of the most important months of her life.

A Pair of Flat Feet
Alison Leonard

As soon as I saw the Head Teacher I knew what he was thinking.

"We'll be delighted to have Tom. Yes, yes." His office was poky and piled high with papers and books. The man himself looked as if he'd been eating too many chips. His eyebrows were like startled bushy caterpillars.

"We're ever so grateful," my mother gushed.

The Head was flicking agitatedly through the papers on his desk. Surely *he* couldn't be nervous? "We have had boys from the Drummond School before," he said, then added, "occasionally!"

"Gym – these lads tend to do well at gym. But no team sports, of course, what with their doing the dancing. Tell me, how was it he took up ... er, ballet?"

He got the whole story from Mum. Me having flat feet when I was at junior school; how the doctor said exercise would cure it; how Gran played the piano for Mrs Lamont's little dancing classes in the village hall – "Not just the Highland dancing, either, but real ballet steps, and even some tap!" And how, after the very first lesson, they could hardly tear me away.

She was so proud of me. Embarrassingly proud. I could see the Head looking at her and, yes, I knew exactly what he was thinking. That he'd rather be dead than have a son like me.

Well, I thought, he's not the first and won't be the last. I knew the whole school would think much the same thing.

It wasn't too difficult at first. This Edinburgh comprehensive was enormous; three times as big as the Academy back home that my village friends were going to. But I had to put up with that. The others in my class didn't ask where I went after school. It didn't occur to them I might not go home at half-three like them. I was determined not to tell them about boarding at the Drummond. If I was a dancer, if I was dedicated to dancing – *addicted* to it – well, that was my private business, no one else's.

There was just one lad, though, who looked as if he might cause me trouble. He was called Bobby Hamilton.

You know how most boys, when they go up to secondary school, are tiny and weedy compared with girls of the same age? At the Drummond School of Dance, all six girls in my Modern group were half a head taller than me. Some of them were "developing", as Miss Grant pointed out. "Gerrells," she'd say, giving *girls* a full two syllables, "let's hope ye don't *develop* over-much. It would ruin your career as a dancer."

When it was my turn to "develop", I'd be going into a jock-strap. Lads who don't dance don't understand. They always make foul jokes about the jock-straps. In fact, it means far less to a boy dancer than starting to wear a bra does to a girl. But what would a lad like Bobby Hamilton say about it?

It wasn't that he was a monster. He wasn't any bigger than most of the girls. But he had such wide shoulders, such a square jaw, and such a long stride as he walked. He expected everyone to turn and look at him. The trouble was, they usually did! And he had a way of staring at girls. Not as if he fancied them, but as if he could see their every weakness.

And that's just how he looked at me.

But at the Drummond it was great. Afternoons, evenings except for homework, most of Saturday and Sunday – dancing, dancing, dancing. *Modern* was my favourite. *Isolations*, when you move different parts of your body separately from the rest. The jazz rhythms. Running in rhythm and getting it right at last, jumping, throwing your head. This was what I'd left home for. This was what Gran and Grandad had cashed in their savings for. This was what life was all about.

"Stre-e-e-tch the Achilles!" called Miss Grant. "You're looking like a *gorrrr-illa*, Heather! *Head*, swirrrl . . . Catriona, let's not wear wellington *boots*! Dramatic! It's about *drama*, gerrells and boys . . . stretch, Tom . . ."

At night, I shared a dormitory with four other boys who were also studying dance at the Drummond. I had no brothers or sisters so I'd never had to share a room before. But I needn't have worried. We all needed one another's support and were soon great friends.

The Drummond had originally been set up as an all-girls school of Dancing and Education. Then they realised someone had to train the next Nureyev or Wayne Sleep and they began to take in a few boys each year. But they shipped them out to local schools during the day. To toughen them up, I suppose – give them contact with "ordinary" boys. Boys like Bobby Hamilton!

I was only the one who went to the comprehensive. Duncan and the others at the Drummond couldn't imagine how I coped there on my own. "What d'you say when they call you namby-pamby, mummy's boy?"

"No problem," I said, confidently. "No one knows I'm training at the Drummond."

"It won't last," said Duncan. "Just you wait."

I didn't believe him. Until one break-time, about three weeks into term.

Bobby Hamilton never rushed out like the rest. He sauntered. On this Monday, he sauntered over to my desk where I was putting maps away in my Geography folder. For an ominous moment he just stood, staring at me.

"Saw these poofters in town Saturday," he said. "From the top of a bus."

"Oh?" I said. I heard my voice sounding strong, but my heart was knocking. "How d'ye know they were poofters? And so what, if they were?"

Bobby Hamilton didn't like being spoken back to. His jaw stuck out even more squarely. "Pranced around on tiptoe," he said. "Waved their fingers around like knitting needles."

"Maybe they were jugglers," I said and stood up, shoving folders in my school rucksack. "Or unicycling fire-eaters flexing their muscles."

He took a step towards me. Kept his voice ever so pleasant. "They weren't, ye know. They were about your size," he said, lifting up his finger and thumb to show just how tiny that was. "Fact, there was one of them the spittin' image of ye!"

"Oh?" I said, wandering away by this time. Suddenly, I knew what to do.

"Most likely he *was* like me," I said. "They'll be Drummond boys. That'd be my brother."

"What?" He gripped my shoulder. "Dinnae walk off when I'm talking to ye," he said.

I swung round, my heart beating more normally now. There was something very reassuring about having muscles that no one suspected. I knew I could stand up to Bobby Hamilton. And I knew how.

"My twin brother," I said, airily. "Sam."

"Twin?"

"Aye. You know the Drummond? Sam's an ace dancer. You should see him leap two metres high in the air."

It warmed my heart to see that jaw drop. I'd won

91

the first round of my match with Bobby Hamilton.

No. Sam, my hastily invented twin brother, had won it.

Within a day, everyone in our year knew about Sam. Girls came up to me and said, "Does your brother wear a G-string?" Boys I hardly knew laughed as they went by, "*Swan Lake* – men in tights!" But I was thrilled to bits with myself for inventing Sam. I didn't care. It wasn't me they were sneering at. They could sneer all they liked at Sam.

Bobby Hamilton never said anything. He'd just walk over in my direction, then wander past as if deep in thought.

The thing about being a dancer is, you learn to watch. You watch other people, you watch yourself. It's like having a spare eye that's a fly on the wall. A camera, almost. When the computer gangs swapped disks and argued strategies, I'd see them as if they were the rival gangs in *Romeo and Juliet*. Mr Carmichael bustling round at the end of a lesson, he looked like Doctor Coppélius dusting the dolls. If I needed to go to the Head of Year to explain what sports I could and couldn't do, I was like a fly on the ceiling watching the way I moved towards her, how I stood, what kind of a figure we made.

As Bobby Hamilton moved around me, saying nothing, I knew that he was watching me, just as I was watching him. What I couldn't tell, though, was what his plot was. If this was a ballet scenario, it was one that wasn't written yet.

Might he try and trip me up? I'd have to be careful. Assembly. I thought I was safe in assembly because there were so many people about.

I should have realised. It's the crowd scenes where anything can happen.

One morning, old Caterpillar Eyebrows was lecturing us about something. Litter, I expect. I wasn't listening. I was scribbling a note to my neighbour: *Got the answer to question 5 of Maths homework? I can't make it out!*

I didn't realise that Bobby Hamilton was sitting just behind us. Suddenly, his chin was leaning on my shoulder. "Poor wee poofter can't do his Maths homework!" he whispered. "Poor wee diddums!"

The litter lecture was over. We stood up and everyone started shuffling out. Just as we moved off, Bobby tried to give me a shove with his elbow. But I spotted it in time and skipped out of the way. The girl behind me got it in the ribs instead. I turned, the girl stumbled. Next thing I knew, I was writhing on the floor in excruciating pain. My ankle felt as if it was on fire. I'd actually heard the bone snap.

Did Bobby mean to do that to me? Maybe not. But as two teachers carried me out of the room, I caught sight of the expression on his face – somewhere between a gloating smirk and grin of triumph.

"A clean break," they said at the hospital as they

slapped on plaster. "No gym or sport for at least a month," said the school nurse. "Lucky it didn't happen to your twin brother at that dancing place."

Even she knew about Sam. No one suspected there wasn't a Sam.

Unless, Bobby Hamilton . . .? Right from the start there'd been a knowing look in his eye.

"Well, then," he said, when I hobbled in on my pot leg for the first time. "If it was ye'self that was the dancing boy, wouldn't that just have spoilt your chances?"

I had to hobble around on that pot leg for four weeks. I nearly died of frustration at the Drummond. I had to sit at the back of Duncan's group, doing upper-body movements and watching. The worst thing of all was, it knocked me out of the Christmas show. We were doing *Petrushka* – my favourite.

When I phoned Mum, I could hear her crying on the other end. She missed me terribly, she said. I missed her, too, but you have to put up with things like that if you're going to be a dancer. "No *Petrushka*! And a broken ankle! Oh Tom," she said. "To think it all started with the doctor telling me you'd got two flat feet!"

"Well," I said, "I've certainly got one flat foot now."

At school, everyone was scribbling mottos on my plaster. Bobby Hamilton wrote something round the back. It was night before I had a chance to twist round to read it.

He'd scrawled, *Will I sign your fancypants wee brother's pot leg as well, then?*

So, now I knew he knew.

One afternoon I suspected he was following me home. He lived in the opposite direction. In fact, no one else lived as far out as the Drummond. So I usually spent the last two stops on the bus alone. I'd always sat upstairs at the front of the double-decker bus. Even with my leg in plaster, I still hobbled up the stairs.

It was just possible that Bobby Hamilton might think he could catch my bus, and sit downstairs without me seeing him.

It was crazy, I argued to myself. What'd be the point? Was he trying to get proof that Sam didn't exist? *He'll not get the better of me*, I thought. *I'll not let him crawl inside my head.*

I decided to come down from the top deck of the bus halfway through my ride. I didn't know quite what I'd do if I saw Bobby Hamilton sitting inside.

I held on tight to the rail as I negotiated my pot leg down the stairs. Then, without glancing inside to see who might be sitting there, I sat down on one of those seats that faces the aisle.

Bobby Hamilton was sitting two rows along. He hadn't noticed that I'd sat down behind him.

The stop before mine, I asked the woman in front of me to nudge him.

Bobby turned round. His face was a picture.

"Get off at my stop?" I said. "I'll show you where I live."

"Er . . . I'm going on to my gran's," he said. "I always do on a . . . a Thursday."

"Go on, she'll not miss you for five minutes. Ye can catch the next bus," I said.

"Er . . . all right."

"Ye can meet Sam," I added.

Bobby stared like he'd never stared before.

The conductor was up on the top deck when I pulled the bell for my stop. I was often the only one getting off there. As the bus drew up, I got ready to manoeuvre myself off on to the pavement. Bobby Hamilton didn't stand up. Would he follow me, or not?

It took me a while to get carefully off the bus. The conductor waited. As I hobbled away, I glanced back to see what Bobby was doing. I heard the conductor ting the bell, then saw Bobby rush to the door. The bus jerked into motion. Bobby fell through the door just before it closed, and on to the pavement.

His face looked just like I guess mine must have done in that assembly. In agony.

I hobbled to help him. A passer-by went to ring for an ambulance. It was his ankle, I could see that. It was just like mine, only his was the right one and mine was the left. Unbelievable.

I said to him, as he was wheeled off to the plaster

room, "Shame, your chances are spoilt now, too. Just when I was going to get Sam to teach you some dancing."

Bobby was off school on the Friday. But come Monday he was back, pot-legged just like me. He grimaced at me, I grinned back at him. But, even though people made every kind of joke about us, we didn't say a word to each other.

When everyone was signing Bobby's plaster, I waited around till the end. Then I hobbled over. "Going to your gran's?" I knew that Bobby's gran who lived out beyond the Drummond didn't exist any more than my twin brother Sam.

"Um, no," he said, and nodded towards his pot leg.

"Come on my bus anyway," I said. I scribbled on the plaster, and he leaned over to see what I'd written. *Come and meet my fancypants wee brother.*

He looked up, amazed. "Why? Why'd I want to meet him?"

"'Cos I'm inviting you," I said. "Suit yourself."

He'd learnt to hobble pretty fast and was at the bus stop before me. We did the whole journey without saying a word.

As we hobbled up the Drummond School drive Bobby looked distinctly uncomfortable – somewhere between fascinated and wishing he was on a different planet.

I took him straight to where Miss Grant would be

doing Modern Dance with Duncan and his group. Duncan had grown faster and was far stronger than the rest of the boys. Already, Miss Grant could imagine him lifting the "gerrells".

The girls and Duncan laughed as we hobbled in. "This is Bobby Hamilton," I said to them. "We've got a lot in common." Bobby didn't like being laughed at by girls, or by a tall poofter in tights. I just wanted to see his face when Duncan started his elevations.

I got my reward.

Bobby was gobsmacked. It was twenty minutes before he uttered a sound.

Then he started muttering to me while Miss Grant was showing Morag how to slide forward on her little finger. "How's he do it? Look at his muscles! Do they ever measure how high he jumps?"

I didn't think he needed answers. "D'ye want to see my fancypants wee brother, then?"

"Aye, where is he?"

"He's away. He'll be back next week."

"When ye've got that pot leg off?"

"Aye, that's right," I said.

"He's yoursel', is he not?" said Bobby.

I nodded. "The *poofter*!" I suddenly wanted to ask him something, so I did. "What d'ye reckon by *poofter*? What would ye say it is?"

"Ye ken fine what it is," said Bobby, and he coughed. Then he said, "Are ye one?"

"Couldn't say. Are you?"

"Ach, drop it," he said. "Where d'ye stay? Where's the rest of the classes? Do they all of them fly around like that? D'ye do five hundred press-ups a day, or what?"

I showed him round the whole school. When he saw our five-bedded dormitory, he couldn't believe it. "D'ye not go home to you mam?" And he didn't once stare at the girls. No, I tell a lie. He stared once. Morag just stared back at him, and he dropped his eyes.

"Hey," I said eventually, feeling really relaxed. "Did you ever have flat feet?"

"Aye, I did at my first school," said Bobby.

"So did I," I said. "We make a right, pair, d'ye not think?"

All around the school hung posters for *Petrushka*. I didn't say it was my favourite. It was bad enough being out of the show because of my ankle, without having Bobby Hamilton say, "Lucky beggar, ye managed to get out of that fancypants wee show, anyway."

But, just as we were hobbling back down the drive, he said, "This Christmas thingie you're putting on. Are ye not going to get your mates up here to the Drummond to see ye? Will ye try and grab me a front seat?"

CÉCILE
Rachel Leyshon

For all of my eighteen years I have lived at the court of King Louis XIV and for the first ten of those years I believed it to be a glittering, promising place. But it has disintegrated before my eyes and, indeed, very little remains of the golden kingdom that I once knew. Now, it gives me a sour taste in my mouth – like chewing lemon rind. I would rather be one of the peasants that stretch their raw, red hands through the front gate for scraps of food. And it is ballet that has opened my eyes to the real world. Because of ballet I have learnt that life is a deception – which, in French, means disappointment.

My mother is a lady-in-waiting. My father is a courtier. We live in the palace at Versailles, just outside Paris, with other courtly and *gentil* people. We have a sumptuous apartment overlooking the world-famous palace gardens and I have a particular window seat where I often curl up to watch the ladies and gentlemen of the court parade and preen themselves amongst the summer flowers. Fortunately, the length of the heavy draped curtains hides me from view, because it is not done to be seen doing nothing. I am generally expected to sit up straight on a delicate chair, work my tapestry and copy the manners of the older ladies. For this is to be my profession. I am to be a lady-in-waiting. And until one February day, eight years ago now when the air was light and chilled grey,

I had thought of being nothing else.

I was ten. I had a best friend whose name was Louis. He was thirteen. His parents had named him after the King and whenever he said his name he looked a little shy as though he wasn't big enough to wear it. He had brown coffee-coloured eyes, fringed with long black lashes. Secretly, I thought he was good-looking. However, he had a lisp and his parents shouted at him whenever he said *th'il vous plaît* instead of *s'il vous plaît* because it meant that he could never be the perfect courtier they wanted him to be.

"What is a courtier anyway?" I remember asking Louis one day as we were playing croquet on the lawn. "What do they do?"

"Well," said Louis carefully, "they have to ride, fence and dance." (He said *fenth* and *danth*.) "But you also have to compose poetry and music and woo ladies. It's best if you serenade them under their windows at night."

He scratched his head. "I think."

"Oh," I said and knocked his red croquet ball out of the game into the flowerbed. I giggled at his crestfallen face. Louis didn't like losing but then neither did I.

It had been, as I said, a clear February day and there was a strong wind which rumbled through the bare trees and spun the enormous skirts of the ladies-in-waiting. There was a rumble of excitement inside the palace too. Eyes were bright and everyone seemed in a hurry to get their work done early. I was in hiding behind the curtain, amusing myself by watching the busy court. Maman's high-pitched voice shattered my day-dreams.

"Cécile! Cé-ciile!"

I ran from my perch on the window seat to her salon. I remember that my father was there, too, which was unusual. He placed a hand on my head. It was a touch as light as air. Like his step. He floated through my life like a wish. His whole being was light and his eyes were dreamy. Maman was sharper, like a little bird.

"*Ma cherie*," said my mother. "Tonight there is a ball to celebrate the return of the King to Versailles. There is to be a spectacle too, a new ballet, *and* the King is dancing. Soooo exciting! Now, please, go and put on your dress. The blue one. Try and be quick and then I will do your hair. That'll take long enough. *Allez! Vite, vite, vite!*"

I wasn't excited, although Maman was chivvying and cheeping like an Easter chick. Louis and I had planned a midnight feast. We'd filched scraps from the busy kitchens. The chefs and kitchen hands had been shouting and clattering. They hadn't noticed us. We had chestnuts and raspberry cordial. I wanted to put the chestnuts in the fire until they split and you could see the cream kernel all tender inside. Instead I would have to sit on a hard chair near my mother and watch some sort of circus. It would be like the acrobats who came to the court once a year with their coloured clothes and monkeys to do backflips and walk on their hands. They brought painted ladies, too, with black eyes and scarlet lips that made my mother sniff with disapproval.

Maman dragged my hair back and I screeched and pulled faces as she tugged her fingers through it. My hair is thick and auburn. Louis, who never used to say anything nice about me, said once that it was beautiful. Another time I caught him staring at it. I have let him brush it, too, although Maman would die if she knew. Anyway, I sat on my hard chair and I had flesh of the goose on my arms because it was cold. Even so, the ladies brought their fans, for show, and peeped round them. I brought mine, too, and made faces at Louis from behind it, which made him laugh. Everyone was seated facing the back of the ballroom and there was a part of the floor that was raised up as a stage.

My father told me that King Louis was called The Sun King ever since he had danced the part of the Sun in a ballet many years ago. Truly, when he entered the stage he did seem to glitter from head to toe. I believed there and then that this man could control the world. The rest of the dancers, who had retired to the back of the stage to make way for him, might have been puppets. His shoes were high-heeled and encrusted in jewels of different colours and shapes. He wore stocking and garters underneath his full shorts, and his wig reached in chestnut curls down to his waist. The feathers on his headdress reached half his height again and they swished and hissed when he inclined his head. His steps were small yet made no sound. His hands moved like mist. But I could not take my eyes from his face. His eyes, which were at once liquid yet hard as little pebbles, appeared to search out the secrets of the whole court. And I, sitting next to Maman, felt as though he could see into my heart.

After the stately minuet came a slow, graceful pavane and he bent at the knees in *pliés* and *fondus* that seemed to melt. He was not a slim man but it did not seem to matter. I was struck dumb and my mother was glad that I had stopped fidgeting. She fanned herself and patted my hand when the King had made his slow exit to the back of the stage where two attendants waited to open and close the doors.

I never saw him dance again.

The next day the court was asleep, almost as if by magic, but more likely sleeping off the effects of the night before. I began to wander on my own through the palace although I knew this was not approved. Children, especially girls, were meant to be kept on a tight rein. Eventually, I found myself in a long hall. The walls were lined with mirrors and there was gold everywhere. The floor was polished with beeswax and it creaked as I put one tentative foot forward.

In the enormous space in front of me I tried to copy some of the dance steps I had seen last night. I had to lift my skirts above my ankles to see if I was doing the right thing.

I looked around, guiltily. "No lady is *ever* to reveal her leg," said Maman in my head. But I did not understand how ladies could know if they were dancing properly if no one could see their legs. They could be rolling about on wheels for all anyone knew.

I pliéd and stretched my legs in front and behind, trying to point my toes. I held my arms out as if balancing them on a huge skirt and I bowed to my reflection in the immense hall. A hundred faces bowed back at me. My audience! I bowed again in a deep reverence and as I did so I heard a step behind me. I whirled round, almost slipping on the polished wood.

"Mademoiselle," said the man at the entrance to the hall. I curtseyed again – a quick bob this time. I knew my face was scarlet. He began to walk towards me. I was in the middle of the hall and it took some time. I thought the creak of the floor under his authoritative step would never stop. He was a tall man and walked with his feet slightly turned out like a duck. He carried his head very high. I recognised him as he approached as Louis' dancing master, Monsieur Beauchamps.

"What are you doing in this part of the palace?"

he said. His dark face was stern and his voice cracked like a whip. "And, furthermore, what were you doing showing your ankles? Shocking, young lady! I've a good mind to have you reported. Eh? What have you got to say for yourself?"

"Pardon … *pardonnez-moi Monsieur*. You see, I was at the ballet last night and … well, I wanted to see if I could do steps like that. And I didn't mean to come here. But I was just wandering and it seemed like just the spot … I …"

I faltered. It was all going wrong. I was in trouble.

"Well, mademoiselle." He stopped for a minute and then my beating heart calmed as I saw him smile. "Ah! Dupont's daughter! Well, well."

"Yes, Monsieur."

"Ah, your father. *Quel danseur! Quel ballon!* A delight to watch …" His eyes beamed for a second and then he continued more sternly.

"Well, now, Mademoiselle Dupont, first you must know that, in ballet, women never do the same thing as the men. For women, the grace is in the movement of the arms and in the poise of the head. But your enthusiasm does you credit and the steps were not perfect but you seem to have a good idea. We could make a good court dancer of you. I'll have a word with your father. Now, get along back to your mother and we'll say no more of this."

I ran through the corridors (this was also forbidden) to the garden where I knew Louis was practising his fencing. A dancer! Me! I signalled to him from behind a bush. "Psssst! Guess what!"

So, I was permitted to take dancing lessons. Three hours a week with Monsieur Beauchamps and ten other girls of about my age. We were told how to keep our shoulders and hips in line, to pull up from the stomach, even though in time we would have to wear corsets which would do half that job. We held our shoulders down, and our heads up, balancing plates or books on them to help us stand elegantly. We made our arms look fluid and graceful by pretending we were immersed in water or by imagining that we were weaving threads around ourselves like a web. We were taught to *plié* without sticking out our *derrières* and how to walk swiftly without seeming to hurry. I learnt how to turn my legs out from the hip and to point my foot without making a sickle shape inwards. I also stopped biting my nails to make my hands look more graceful. "Thank Heaven for ballet," said my mother.

But we were not taught how to dance intricate footwork and we were not allowed to leap. "You are ladies," said Monsieur Beauchamps when I asked him why we could not do these things. "In any case, one does not jump in ballet. And the gentlemen perform the virtuoso footwork. You, the ladies, must embellish their efforts. Who would see your footwork under your cumbersome skirts?"

"Well, shorten them," I said boldly but was silenced by his look of shocked outrage. So I practised these steps on my own and learnt more from Louis when I could.

So the years went by in a succession of bright winters and golden summers at Versailles. Louis became taller than me, suddenly acquired a jaw-line and broad shoulders and I began to wear fuller skirts. We both took our dancing lessons, and the court sculptors worked on a life size stone sculpture of King Louis on his horse to be placed in the courtyard in the entrance to the palace. By the time it was finished Monsieur Beauchamps announced that I had become "an accomplished dancer". But my parents, although pleased with my achievements, refused to send me to the King's dancing "Académie" in Paris, despite my nagging and sulking. I had to be content with hearing about it from Louis when he was allowed to visit his parents at Versailles. He had been sent there when he reached his fourteenth birthday. His parents had decided that with his lisp, dancing was the best career he could possibly hope for. I missed him. There was no one to tell me jokes, to listen to my stories, to laugh at my worries. I always looked forward to the Académie holidays.

"They say that I shall be allowed to perform on the stage after Christmas," Louis told me on one of his visits. It was late October and flocks of migrating birds were gathering like scraps of wire in the troubled autumn sun. We were walking the length of the now bleak winter gardens. Both our parents were strolling behind us but were out of earshot. I was furious with jealousy. To be allowed to dance in the theatre! Zut! I snapped a rose hip from its stem as we walked and twiddled it between my fingers.

"I'm very happy for you, Louis." I said it between gritted teeth. In the next instant I knew I had to leave Versailles. I had to dance and I had to dance in Paris. Once my parents saw me dance there they would be impressed and delighted and proud. They would have no choice but to let me be a professional dancer.

"Louis," I said. "Tell me, when are you going back to Paris? Could you do with a servant to help you with your bags?"

Louis' eyes opened wide with shock. Then he began to laugh, and I knew I had an ally.

"Would I ever leave you?" he said mockingly, and his arm brushed my shoulder, sealing the conspiracy. And then the unsaid words hung between us.

But of course it was a disaster and I was disgraced.

I persuaded Monsieur Beauchamps, now the director of the Académie, that I was in Paris with the full consent of my parents. Delighted, although, he confessed, extremely surprised that my father had allowed it, he gave me a very small part in his New Year ballet. I was fifteen. But for the opportunity to dance once more on the stage, I would suffer double the disgrace that followed.

I could hardly breathe as I stood in the wings listening to the bars of music tick away with the plink of the harpsichord. And when I made my entrance, the lights almost blinded me. I nearly stumbled. But I pulled my shoulders back and lifted my head and bowed and *pliéd* in a familiar pavane. My muscles responded in the way they had been trained. I caught Louis' eye as he made his entrance opposite me and we grinned like idiots. I had never felt so happy. It felt so real – Louis and I performing our everyday steps – my arms, my legs, my feet. The comfort of Louis' hand in mine. And yet it was as magical and as cloudy as a dream. Gradually my eyes became used to the bright lights of the stage and the dim lights of the auditorium. Clearer and clearer became the faces of the audience, upturned like gaudy sunflowers. And, as I sank into my final reverence, one face at the back of the theatre became even clearer. My father! I stared at the wooden boards of the stage and willed him to go away or for it really to be a dream. But when I lifted my head and swept off the stage to enthusiastic applause (my first applause!) he was still there, only too real.

Of course, he bundled me into the family carriage, sweeping aside Louis' frantic explanations with a wave of his elegant white hand and we drove at a breakneck speed back to Versailles. I cried all the way home but my father could have been a marble statue in the carriage beside me.

"Young ladies of your upbringing," he said in a voice as hard as diamond, "do not parade themselves on stage for all and sundry to see." He gripped my arm to help me out of the carriage. "Dancing for aristocratic young ladies is an amusement for their cultural well-being, for their health. It is to be partaken with their friends or, at most, in front of the court. A chosen audience. You, my dear, have not been permitted to take ballet lessons in order to show off your skills in front of just anyone, like a common acrobat. There will be no more dancing lessons for you."

And that was that. Three years later I am still only allowed out of my mother's sight to take a walk with an approved lady friend or to play croquet. Louis, I hear, has gone from strength to strength in Paris. He has been made a *danseur noble* (the highest accolade for a male dancer) and has become renowned throughout France. Since that New Year's day when my father's carriage rattled furiously away from the theatre leaving Louis a tearful smudge in the clear winter air, I have not been allowed to keep in touch with him. If there have been letters from him they have been hidden or destroyed.

I saw him for the first time in three years at the

May ball in Paris a month ago. He entered the room and was soon surrounded by a large excited and chattering group. People craned their necks to look at him and murmured as he passed. Without a thought, I skipped across the room.

"Cécile!" hissed my mother but I didn't care.

I joined the chattering throng and, despite disapproving looks, I edged my way to the middle of the circle that had closed in around Louis. As I ducked by the final person I dislodged my heavy coiffure. The weight of it knocked me off balance and I fell forward on to the now famous instep of my Louis. I looked up, giggling, but instead of the grin I knew so well, I found myself gazing into a cold glare that, without a shadow of a doubt, did not recognise me.

"Madame," he said as I began to apologise, "quite thimply you have put all of Paris in mourning for a week."

And he swept past me in a waft of admirers, flowers and perfume.

But I am not in the least surprised that he did not know me. Really. My hair had been elaborately coiffured on top of my head, my face heavily powdered, my waist squeezed in to the regulation thirteen inches by my corset. In his eyes I was just another clumsy devotee who might have injured his valuable feet. I can quite see that.

And so here I am. A lady-in-waiting now, at the

beginning of my court career. Outside, the June air smells fresh and lemon-bitter and I sit upright on my fine chair, working my tapestry with the other ladies. On a fine chair opposite me sits a young girl. She keeps looking out of the window and pricking her thumbs by mistake. Sometimes I notice her copying my gestures.

FLAIR
Alison Prince

With her hand on the bedroom windowsill as a *barre* (although it was quite a lot too low), Tashi was secretly doing some late-night ballet practice. *Pliés* in first position: slow, back straight, the free arm sweeping down as the knees bent. Then the same in second: feet apart, turned out as if standing on an imaginary straight line. Shoulders down, don't look agonised. A dancer must never show any sign of strain, Miss Martin said, or the whole thing is ruined.

Third. Fourth. Then the difficult fifth, in which the feet are crossed and lie close, one in front of the other. Hard to keep the hips turned out so that the front foot didn't roll forward. Tashi glanced at her lamp-lit reflection in the dressing-table mirror that showed only her top half, and felt the usual discontent. She looked plain and schoolgirlish, even though she had put on her leotard and scraped her hair back into a rubber band. Her face was so depressingly *round*.

Never mind. Keep going. It was the exam on Saturday week, no time to lose. *Battements tendus.* Working leg extended to the front, swept round to the side and then the back, not lifting the foot from the floor. Mustn't make any noise, though. One tell-tale scrape or thump, and Mum would be upstairs in a flash, scolding her for being out of bed. But there was so little time to practise, what with school taking up most of the day and then homework, and being expected to sit in front of the TV with Mum and Dad and Rory, to be sociable. How could a dancer ever succeed in such circumstances?

Battements fondus. Float, Miss Martin said. Keep the movement soft and fluid. *Fondre* means to melt. Place the foot above the other ankle, bend the knee of the supporting leg, straighten as the working foot goes forward, then out, then back, with the arm following the movement. Tashi was a little out of breath now, her heart beating fast, and she hadn't even started the other *battements* or the *développés* which demanded the slow unfolding of the leg to its furthest extent. That was the one that made your thigh muscles feel as if they were on fire. You should never do the exercises out of their proper order, Miss Martin said. But it really was getting late. Perhaps it wouldn't matter, just this once, to skip the *développés* and do some stretches instead.

Prop the foot on the windowsill, slide it along, leaning over it, holding the ankle, touch the head on the knee—

With a proper *barre* it would never have happened. The indignant thought flashed through Tashi's head even as her foot slipped and she crashed to the floor. She sat on the carpet, trying not to sob, nursing the side of her face which had hit the corner of the dressing table as she fell. Downstairs, the door of the sitting room opened. Tashi scrambled awkwardly to her feet as her mother came running upstairs.

"Na-*tasha*!" She only used Tashi's full name when she was cross. "It's gone eleven o'clock. What on earth are you doing?"

"I just ... needed to get some practice in." Tashi fought back tears. Her left eye hurt sharply from the collision.

Her mother gave an irritable sigh as she stood in the doorway, small and neat and angry. "I sometimes wish I'd never let you start these dancing lessons. Ballet's not the only thing in the world, you know."

It is, it is, Tashi protested silently. You don't understand.

"What have you done to your face?" Her mother approached and put her hand under Tashi's chin to look at the already red and swollen eye.

"I just ... slipped."

Another sigh, a tired one this time. "What *am* I to do with you? Go and bathe it with some cold water, for goodness' sake. Not that it'll do much good. You'll have an absolute shiner by the morning."

She was right. The next day, Tashi's eye was puffy and half-closed, a dark purple colour. At school, everyone thought it was very funny. Miriam was the only one who sympathised. But then, Miriam was mad about ballet, too, and she understood how vital it was to put in all the practice you could, especially in the last few days before an exam.

"If I'd been working at a proper *barre* it would never have happened," Tashi lamented, and Miriam nodded agreement. "I don't even have any space between the wall and my bed," she said. "I was trying to do a *rond de jambe en l'air* the other day, and knocked the bedside lamp over. Hopeless."

The pair of them were sitting in the cloakroom during a wet lunch hour. Moodily, Tashi got up and stretched her arms above her head, clenched fists close together, full of impatience and frustration. The movement caused a throbbing in her injured eye, so she transferred her attention to her feet, moving restlessly through the five positions.

Miriam, still sitting, obligingly extended her own foot to nudge Tashi's toe back into the proper line. "Fifth is so vital, isn't it," she said. "I mean, you need it for the *échappés* and the *soubresauts* and everything."

Tashi did a couple of sketchy *demi-pliés* then sat down again, knees out like the girls in the Degas paintings, hands slack in her lap. Ordinary people didn't know the pain at the top of the thighs or the desperation of wanting to get it right. Most of them would never feel that magical lift of the heart at sensing what "line" meant, that lovely moment of extending into the space beyond you. That's why you had to "look through the wall", as Miss Martin said. So that you weren't contained by the room but in touch with something bigger – the spirit that

124

lay in the music and the dance. And once you knew that sensation, it was as if there was a clarity inside you, and all you had to do was get rid of the weakness and clumsiness and let it shine through. But you had to be tough with yourself, otherwise you'd never be anything more than most of Miss Martin's pupils. Just little girls who fancied themselves looking pretty in tutus even if they had no more idea of line than a guinea pig.

"I think I'm too fat," she mourned now, stretching out a leg. Miss Martin's legs were so lean that you could see every strand of muscle move.

"No, you're not," Miriam said. "And at least you're the right height. I'm going to grow too big, I know I am. Just look at the size of my feet. I take five-and-a-half already, and my mother keeps saying I ought to wear sixes. I won't though, I absolutely refuse to."

"They won't grow any more now we're on points," Tashi assured her, secretly crossing her fingers in case this was not true. And then the bell rang, and she and Miriam trailed off to Maths.

While Mr O'Hare went through something to do with triangles, Tashi found herself thinking about her mother. She did this quite often, though not because she really wanted to. It was more like a nagging headache that came of its own accord. Her mother was such a puzzle. The dancing classes had been her idea in the first place. "They'd be good for Tashi's posture," she had said, nodding her dark head with its neatly cropped hair that curved into points on her cheeks. Every girl should do some ballet. She'd seemed so keen on it. When she came to meet Tashi from the class and stood talking to Miss Martin, she looked like a dancer herself, slim and precise with her hands loosely clasped in front of her. And she knew about ballet. She'd spotted Zoë Levinson straightaway. "That girl has flair," she'd said. But then, everyone notice Zoë. Who wouldn't? She was as light and red-haired and brilliant as a firefly.

Flair. Tashi pondered this as she wrote letters in the corners of her triangles. Did you have to be born with flair, or was it something you could develop? Her mother had it, that was for sure. She was as sleek and self-possessed as a black cat. Her grandfather had been Russian; that's why she had called her daughter Natasha. Tashi was proud of all that. Inwardly, she felt that she, too, had flair, that she was special, with a fire of feeling inside her that demanded a special control. She sighed, rubbing out an x and replacing it with a y. Her mother obviously thought she had no flair at all. Her enthusiasm for the ballet classes had ebbed away and changed to irritation. It could only mean that she, Tashi, was no good. Her mother was disappointed in her.

Miss Martin was not too concerned about Tashi's black eye. "Don't worry about that. You'll be wearing make-up for the exam. It'll never show. And there's a whole week to go before next Saturday. But you must be careful," she added. "What if you'd broken an ankle? Then you'd be in real trouble. You're better to use the back of a chair for practice, like we do here if there are too many for everyone to get on the *barre*. Windowsills are very treacherous."

"Yes," said Tashi. But the chair in her room was a dumpy upholstered thing, not a bit like the sturdy wooden ones Miss Martin used. And she could hardly go marching into the kitchen and take one; her mother would only want to know what it was for.

No time to think about it now. Miss Martin had gone to the centre of the room and clapped her hands, and Mrs Ollershaw at the piano had begun the rippling arpeggio which accompanied the formal curtsey to begin the class. *Barre* work first, then centre practice, followed by *jetés* across the room and pirouettes, then the country dance. Tone and rhythm exercises, clapping the patterns played by Mrs Ollershaw, then the free interpretation, which was Tashi's favourite. This week, it was a mechanical little tune with a sadness in its gaiety that was difficult to interpret. Tashi pranced to the four-square rhythm like an obedient pony, lifting her

knees high, but letting her arms hang limply by her sides and her head loll as if oppressed by secret sorrow.

"Now, what do you think that was?" Miss Martin asked when the music stopped. Several people said it was a march. Zoë, with the slimness of her long legs muffled in pale blue leg-warmers, suggested that it might be about a clown. "Very nearly," said Miss Martin. "It's called *Puppet's Complaint*, by César Franck. A puppet is a prisoner, you see, in spite of seeming so lively. It's helpless in the hands of whoever pulls the strings. Tashi, will you show us what you did? I think you sensed the mood of the music very well."

And so Tashi danced on her own while everyone watched. With her head tilted to the right, she knew that her bruised eye added its own poignancy to the helplessness she was evoking.

Zoë watched with her arms folded and her face expressionless, and Tashi was careful not to look at her. Zoë didn't like anyone else to be in the limelight.

The class ended with the set dance they would be doing for the exam, but on the way home on the bus, the puppet tune still echoed in Tashi's mind. Sometimes she felt that she, too, was a puppet, attached by strings to the routine of school. Later, there would be other strings as she went obediently to college and to some sort of job. It was a depressing thought.

Ballet was different. It, too, had strict demands, but at the end of your training, ballet would give you the freedom to express your real self, as well as all the passion and excitement you could find in the music. Performing like this for an audience would let them, too, feel the magical prickling of gooseflesh on the back of the neck. It was a thing you would never lose. Tashi had seen a film of Alicia Markova, grey-haired, in a jersey and skirt, working with Royal Ballet students, and the magic was still there, still as beautiful.

On the morning of the exam, Tashi sat in the back of the car beside Miriam, praying that she hadn't forgotten anything. New satin shoes, darned across the toes for grip, scissors to cut the ribbons once they'd been tied, regulation tights, white leotard with its little skirt, hair spray, pins and hair net for making a neat, wisp-free bun, sweater for warm-up. Her mother was driving, and Miriam's mother sat beside her, talking about patio doors. She was a big woman, very kind and cheerful, and very un-ballet.

When they arrived, the changing room was already full of girls and one or two boys, all with their mothers. Throughout the journey, Tashi had been almost sick with terror that they'd be late. "For goodness' sake," her mother had snapped, "I do *know* what the time is, Tashi. There's no point in getting there too early."

Miss Martin was looking elegant in a scoop-necked black dress, with a large towel pinned round her waist because she was putting on people's make-up. Teachers were being extremely calm and the boys, in tunics and tights, were trying to look reserved and lofty in spite of the eye-shadow.

Zoë was in tears. Her hands fluttered pathetically as other people's mothers offered hankies and words of comfort. Her own mother was nowhere to be seen. "I'm going to fail," she wept. "I know I am. My mind's gone blank, I can't remember anything."

Tashi and Miriam exchanged glances. Zoë was always like this before exams.

The door opened and a woman with a clipboard called in the first pair of candidates – two from another school. Tashi caught a glimpse of the vast, brightly-lit floor and the grand piano. So did Zoë, and cried even harder. "Totally hysterical," said Tashi's mother with distaste. "Who's supposed to be looking after her?"

"I think her mum's gone out for a cigarette," said Miriam. "She said she wanted a breath of fresh air."

At that moment, Mrs Levinson came in. She had the same red hair as her daughter, but she was quite fat and wore a lot of lipstick. She marched across to Zoë, yanked her to her feet and shook her, hard. "Stop that at once!" she commanded. "Just *look* at your make-up. Here—" She grabbed a tissue from the nearest hand. "Blow your nose." Zoë blotted and blew and sniffed. "You and Annette are the next pair in," her mother went on, "and you're to smile, do you hear me? Go in there and *smile*." Amazingly, Zoë smiled, tremulous and tear-stained but with a curve to her parted lips that had a ghostly gaiety about it. "Powder puff," said her mother with a click of her plump fingers, and Miss Martin stepped forward to powder Zoë's nose, trying hard to suppress her amusement.

When they were called in, Zoë's head was held high, her smile radiant. Her mother gave a little sigh and said, "I was like that myself. Full of temperament. Fruit-drop, anyone?"

Tashi thought afterwards that the exam had been like a dream. Chandeliers, long mirrors in which she and Miriam were reflected with dazzling clarity, winter trees outside the windows, a strange pianist at the great black piano (and strange playing that made all the tempi seem different), and the judges behind their baize-covered table. The free interpretation had been difficult, all little runs and pauses as if you were frightened of something. And then there was the long wait while all the other pairs went in. Time to change, comb out the stiffness of hair spray, take off the make-up, go to the loo, try not to think about the coming result.

At last Miss Martin came in, together with the other teachers, all of them with mark-sheets and all smiling. The candidates clustered around them. "Everyone's passed," Miss Martin said. "There are four credits, to Claire, Annette, Pauline and Miriam. And Zoë and Tashi both have Distinction."

Zoë promptly burst into tears again, and so did Miriam because she'd only got a credit. The boys were grinning, people were hugging each other. Mrs Levinson produced a huge box of chocolates from her capacious bag and Zoë, with a perfect curtsey in spite of her blotched eyes, gave it to Miss Martin amid enthusiastic applause.

Tashi's mother put on her coat, turning up its fur collar. Her face looked very pale against its darkness. "Better be getting home, I think," she said. Like Zoë, she smiled, but Tashi saw that it was a smile full of sadness.

In bed that night, Tashi wept. Zoë was so lucky, having a mother who understood what ferocity and love dancing demanded; one who could turn up with chocolates tied with a red bow so that the proper gesture could be made. No wonder Zoë had flair. Compared with Mrs Levinson, Tashi's own mother was as indifferent and self-possessed as the little black cat she resembled. And yet – Tashi wept afresh to think of it – her mother was so much more beautiful than Mrs Levinson. There was a quickness and fire about her dark eyes and neat head that made Tashi feel she owed her passion for ballet to her mother. And yet – it all seemed so hopeless.

Choking with sobs, she did not hear the quiet footsteps that came up the stairs, and when light from the landing flooded in through her bedroom door, it was too late to pretend.

Her mother sat down on the bed beside her. Tashi turned her head away. She couldn't stop crying. Her hair was being stroked. She could smell her mother's faint perfume, hear the little sigh she gave. "It's the dancing, isn't it? Tashi, I'm so sorry."

"You want me to give it up, don't you?" Tashi blurted. "You don't think I'm any good, I can see, you're always so—" Words failed her.

"Oh, darling." They were in each other's arms.

"I can't give it up, Mum," Tashi wept. "I just can't. You don't understand."

"I do understand, my love. I understand all too well."

Tashi looked up through her tears and saw that her mother's eyes, too, glistened with sadness. "Mum? What is it?"

Her mother reached for a tissue from the box on the dressing table, and in that moment, Tashi knew. Only a dancer could extend an arm quite like that, the elbow soft, the lovely line going through and beyond the outstretched hand. "Were you—?"

"Yes, I was a dancer. Or very nearly. I'd auditioned for the Royal Ballet School. They seemed pleased. I thought I was going to get in. Then I broke my ankle."

Tashi gasped. Miss Martin's warning was clear in her mind. "*Then you'd be in real trouble.*"

"Such a silly thing, too," her mother went on. "At a party, playing Murder in the Dark. I fell over the back of a sofa, we were all fooling about. It didn't set quite right. Haven't you noticed?"

She switched on the bedside light, and in the sudden glare Tashi peered at the foot her mother extended, neat in its suede shoe. Was the ankle fractionally thickened? Not that anyone could see. But for ballet, where they even X-ray your joints to see if you are the kind who grows too big – no chance.

"How *awful*," Tashi said.

"Yes, I was unlucky. But you see, darling, dancing's so full of disappointments. I wanted you to have the experience of it. I think every girl should do at least some. It's so good for you. But I didn't want you to fall in love with it. So few girls ever become professional dancers, even in the *corps de ballet*. It's so physically hard. And failure is so shattering."

"I know." Tashi took a deep breath, trying to steady her voice. "Mum, I won't ever be a ballerina. I know that. I'm not looking for flowers and fame and everything. I just … want to dance. To do it properly." It was the first time Tashi had put this in to words, and there was a sadness in knowing she would not move with the moonlit-silver girls in *Swan Lake* or join in the Russian fire of *Petrushka*. But she was her own person, not a puppet to do what other people expected. "If I could be as good as Miss Martin – and hand it on, teach other people who might not ever get to know it otherwise ..." Her words petered out.

Her mother hugged her again, rocking very slightly. Tashi felt her limbs slacken as the tensions of the day ebbed in this new comfort. She was hardly aware of being tucked in, and of the room's return to darkness.

A few days later, it was Tashi's birthday. There were cards at breakfast time, and Rory gave her a jigsaw with a scene from *Coppélia* on it, but there was nothing else. Her parents kept giving each other little smiles. Some plan was afoot, that much was clear. "Your present from us will be here this afternoon," her father said as he tucked his mobile phone into his jacket pocket. "Must fly. Have a lovely day, pet."

School dragged even more than usual, but at last Tashi was letting herself in through the back door at quarter past four that afternoon.

"There you are!" said her mother. "Come and see what we've got for you." Mystified, Tashi followed her mother upstairs. "Look!" And she threw open Tashi's bedroom door.

In that first moment, Tashi saw only that the bed

had been moved and there was more space. More light – a big mirror on the wall. And—

"Oh, Mum," said Tashi. "I don't believe it!" A waist-high *barre* of smooth blond wood ran the whole length of the wall. She walked across to it and sketched a *battement*, then flung herself into her mother's arms. "Thank you!"

"It's from your fans," she heard her mother say as they hugged. "Dad and me. You have real flair, my darling, and we're proud of you."

Had there been roses round her feet on the stage of Covent Garden, Tashi could not have felt more warmly applauded, or more loved.

DANCING NANCY
Josephine Feeney

One Saturday, Nancy went to a wedding. Aunty Nuala was getting married. Nancy couldn't stop looking at Nuala's dress as she stood at the front of the church. It had layers and layers of white lace and tiny pearls swinging from each layer.

It was a very long day for Nancy. First of all, she had to sit perfectly still in church during the ceremony. Then she had to stand outside in the freezing cold for even longer, while the photographs were taken. Everyone was looking at the bride and groom and waiting for their turn to smile and say, "Cheese!"

At the wedding reception Nancy had to wait quietly at the table, even after she'd finished eating her dinner. "Can I get down now?" she pleaded.

"No. You'll have to wait until all the speeches are finished," her mother whispered. Nancy groaned. The speeches were long and very, very boring.

In the evening a band started to play. There was a violin, a flute, a guitar and an accordion. "This is better," Nancy said, tapping her foot. The music was irresistible and soon everyone was up and dancing.

Suddenly, the dance floor cleared and the music stopped. Nancy's cousin, Geraldine, had walked into the middle of the room. She was wearing a beautiful green dress with bright swirling patterns. She pointed her toes in their neat black dancing shoes.

She stood totally still, her back straight, looking towards the far end of the room. When the music started again, Nancy watched as Geraldine whirled around the dance floor. Between each few steps she did a lively little hop and then a twist.

All the wedding guests watched in amazement. Geraldine's long, curly, dark hair flew all around her head as she hopped and kicked and skipped in time to the music. Her feet moved lightly and cleverly around the room. Nancy thought it a truly magical sight.

As Geraldine finished dancing, everyone clapped and cheered and whistled. They were so delighted by Geraldine's dancing that the applause went on for ages.

Nancy was amazed. She leapt up and ran over to Geraldine. "I want to do that! Will you teach me to dance like that?" she asked.

"You have to go to classes. Irish dancing classes," Geraldine explained. "I've been going for five years. Ever since I was seven."

"I want to go to Irish dancing classes!" Nancy shouted. "I want to learn how to dance."

She wanted to dance just like Geraldine. To wear a green dress with lovely swirling patterns and smart black dancing shoes. She wanted to hear the people clapping, shouting and whistling for *her* performance.

The following week Nancy started going to Irish dancing classes in the church hall. It seemed a funny place for dancing. There were no musicians or cheering crowds, or pretty green dresses. Only cold floorboards and pale blue walls that smelt of new paint. Mrs Devine, the teacher, welcomed all the new children and asked them to line up.

"First of all, I want you to stand up straight, with your arms by your side. Now, walk around the room without moving your hands and arms." The children did as Mrs Devine directed. "Good!" she said.

"This is a bit boring. We're not even dancing," Nancy whispered as she passed Geraldine on her trip around the hall. Geraldine, who had come to help Mrs Devine, just smiled.

"That's where your hands and arms stay when you're dancing by yourself," Mrs Devine said. Nancy yawned. This wasn't what she had expected, at all. "Now I'd like you to skip around the hall, keeping your back straight the whole time."

"What on earth are we doing this for? It's boring!" Nancy complained as she passed Geraldine again.

"Nancy, remember to keep your back straight," Mrs Devine called from across the hall.

"You'll soon see what it's for," Geraldine said, as Nancy skipped past her a third time.

Before long, parents began to arrive to pick up the dancers at the end of the lesson. Mrs Devine asked the children to demonstrate what they had learnt.

"I'm not sure if I want to go any more," Nancy said to Geraldine as they walked home together.

"Try it again next week," Geraldine urged. "You'll see. It'll get better. You just have to learn how to stand and move properly first."

So Nancy decided to try the dancing classes for one more week.

"Now children, today we're going to learn the reel," Mrs Devine announced. "I want you to hop and then count to seven steps."

All the new boys and girls hopped and counted seven steps as they moved across the hall. "Now, hop again and . . . back, two, three, just like this," Mrs Devine said.

The children copied her movements, remembering to keep their backs straight and their arms still. "Well done!" Mrs Devine exclaimed.

"This is not much better than last week," Nancy whispered to Geraldine. "I want to dance to music, just like you did in your lovely green dress."

"You have to learn to *dance* first," Geraldine said, somewhat exasperated.

Once again, when all the mums and dads arrived to take the dancers home, Mrs Devine asked the children to show them what they had learnt.

Nancy was so bored she only counted six steps instead of seven. It caused all the children to tumble over as they each bumped into one another behind her. They didn't know whether to laugh or be annoyed. Mrs Devine just smiled and said, "Never mind, Nancy."

Before the dancing class left the hall Mrs Devine reminded them to practise their steps at home during the week. "Don't forget, now."

When Nancy walked home with her mother she was very quiet. "What's up?" her mum asked. "You're not normally this quiet."

"I was thinking about the dancing class," Nancy said. "It's a bit boring. There's no music, no lovely green dresses, and no clapping. Just 'do this,' 'do that,' and 'count to seven'!"

"It'll get better each week, you'll see," Mum said. "If you practise, it'll be *much* better."

All week Nancy practised her steps. "Hop . . . one, two, three, four, five, six, seven," she whispered as she stepped carefully across the floor. "Hop, two, three . . . Back, two, three."

"Don't forget to keep your back straight and your arms next to your sides," Nancy's mum reminded her.

"I *am* doing that," Nancy said, a little annoyed

with her mum's interference.

"Most of the time you are, Nancy, but sometimes you look like a tightrope walker with your arms stretched out," her mother said.

Nancy tried again. And again and again. She practised so much that her back and her shoulders, and her arms and legs were all aching. Even her head hurt. Eventually she shouted, "I can do it!"

In class the following week, Mrs Devine was very pleased. So was Geraldine. Waiting for the newcomers to grasp the basics was frustrating.

"Can we have some music now?" Nancy asked. "And the lovely green dress with the swirling patterns?"

"All right, Nancy," Mrs Devine said, laughing as she switched on the tape recorder at the side of the hall. Nancy started to dance. Although there was a great deal to remember, she managed, with her arms by her side, to dance the first part of the reel.

Mrs Devine was so pleased, she asked Nancy if she would like to dance in a festival.

"Ooh . . . yes please!" Nancy squealed. "Will I be able to wear a lovely green dancing dress?"

"Soon . . . but not yet, Nancy," Mrs Devine said. "When you've won your first medal, we'll see about a dress." Nancy was determined to practise every spare moment she had.

The night before the festival, Nancy was so excited

that she could hardly sleep. She thought about each dance. There was so much to remember! "Stand up straight, arms by your side, point your toes, then . . . hop two, three, four, five, six, seven," she said over and over in her mind. "Back two, three, back two, three. Keep in time . . . listen to the music . . . so much to remember."

Then, before she knew it, Nancy was on the stage at the festival along with several other dancers. She waited with her arms firmly pressed to her sides, her back straight and her right toe pointing, ready to dance.

The band sat at the side of the platform. When they started to play Nancy watched for Mrs Devine to wave her group in. They all began to dance. "Hop two, three, four, five, six, seven," Nancy counted to herself. "So much to remember," she whispered. Little by little, Nancy's arms moved away from her sides. She began to look like a tightrope walker, and after a few steps she lost count. Nancy stopped. The band continued to play and other children continued to dance but everyone in the audience seemed to have stopped breathing.

Suddenly, Nancy started to hop and skip and leap about the stage. She didn't count, she didn't even *hear* the music. She was just hopping and skipping and leaping wildly all over the place. The other children stopped dancing and stared in amazement.

"Stop!" commanded Mrs Devine.

"Stop!" shouted Geraldine.

"Stop!" wailed Nancy's mum and dad.

Nancy fell into a heap in the middle of the stage. The band stopped playing and everyone watching looked away. Mrs Devine was horrified. In all her years of teaching, she had never seen a dancer behave like this at a festival.

Nancy started to cry as Geraldine helped her up from the middle of the stage and walked her down to her mum and dad. She felt so foolish and clumsy.

At the end of the festival the judge gave out medals to the winners. Nobody was surprised when Nancy's name was not called out.

Later that evening, Nancy said, "I hate festivals. They're so boring!" Then she said, "And I don't want to go to Irish dancing classes anymore. They're even worse!" Nancy's mum and dad didn't say anything. They just looked at Nancy and shook their heads sadly. It had been a long, difficult day.

Nancy closed her eyes and went to sleep. It had been a bad day. There was simply too much to remember.

The next Friday, Geraldine called round early for Nancy. "Are you coming to Irish dancing?" she asked.

"No," said Nancy firmly. "I'm not going any more. It's boring!" After a pause she added, "And you never get anything! I practised so hard for that festival and I didn't even win a little medal."

Then Nancy noticed that Geraldine was carrying a big parcel. "What's in that?" she asked.

"Oh . . . it's one of my old dancing dresses. I brought it around for you, but you obviously won't need it now."

"Please can I just look at it?" Nancy asked. "Even though I'm not going to Irish dancing anymore."

Geraldine opened the parcel. Inside was the beautiful green dress with lovely, swirling patterns in orange and yellow and blue. In a separate package was a pair of black dancing shoes.

They were perfect for Nancy. She was so excited, she couldn't wait for a chance to wear them. But then . . . Geraldine started to fold the dress neatly. "I'll just pack this away, Nancy," Geraldine said. "After all, you won't need it. Or the shoes. You're not going to Irish dancing any more, and I'm sure there will be someone else who'll need a dancing dress and shoes."

Nancy thought for a moment. The green dress would look so beautiful when she hopped and skipped and kicked around the stage. The black dancing shoes would help her to move lightly and cleverly across the hall at dancing classes.

"I've changed my mind," Nancy said, quickly.

So, Nancy continued to go with Geraldine to Irish dancing classes. Every week, she listened carefully to Mrs Devine as she showed the children how to dance the reel . . . then the jig . . . then the hornpipe.

She watched Mrs Devine's feet flying to the music of the tinny tape recorder as she showed them each dance.

After every lesson, Nancy asked Geraldine, "When can I wear the beautiful green dress?"

Geraldine just said, "Soon . . . but not yet, Nancy."

Over the weeks, slowly and painstakingly, Nancy learned how to hop and skip and dance. At home she practised her steps. She walked proudly around the room, her arms still and her back straight. To a tune in her head, she counted up to seven for the reel. Again and again she tried the fancy hops and heel-kicks of the jig. At last, all the bits fell together. Nancy remembered *everything*.

Nancy was dancing!

A few weeks later, Nancy and her mum and dad were invited to another family party. After the food had been eaten, the band began to play. There was a violin, a flute, a guitar and an accordion.

Geraldine walked into the middle of the room, pointed her toes, and started to dance. She kicked and hopped and leapt all over the room.

Then Nancy's mother whispered, "Here's your lovely green dress with the swirling patterns. Why don't you put it on and dance with Geraldine?"

So Nancy put on her glorious dress and walked

into the middle of the room with Geraldine. When the music started again the two girls stepped and hopped and kicked and leapt all over the room. All the guests were delighted.

When the music finally stopped, everyone clapped and cheered and whistled. Geraldine whispered, "Nancy, it's your turn now. Off you go." Nancy looked petrified. "Don't worry." Geraldine said with an encouraging smile. "Just do the reel and show all your cousins how you can dance."

And she did! Her green dress with the swirling patterns flew around the room as she twirled and kicked and danced in time to the music. "Now, I'm really dancing!" Nancy said to herself. She was *so* happy.

When she finished, the party guests clapped and cheered and whistled. Nancy felt so proud. "One day I'll win a medal, just like Geraldine's!" she thought.

Marie, Nancy's little cousin, was enchanted by the dancing. "Will you teach me how to do that?" she asked Nancy, tugging at her sleeve.

"You have to go to classes – Irish dancing classes. Just like I did," Nancy said proudly.

"Is that all?" Marie said.

"Yes, but it's really hard work! There's so much to remember, but you just have to keep trying and trying."

"And practising," Geraldine added.

"And you must never give up," Nancy said. "Even when you think it's boring, or too hard. Because it's worth it in the end."

"Teach me some now," Marie said, getting excited.

"All right," Nancy agreed. "Keep your back perfectly straight, arms by your side. Now copy me – hop two, three, four, five, six, seven . . ."

And so, as the adults in the lounge started to sing, Nancy, Geraldine and Marie hopped and danced across the kitchen floor. Nancy and Geraldine's dresses with the swirling patterns moved gently.

"When can I wear one of those lovely, green dresses?" Marie asked.

"Not for a long time yet," Nancy said, her eyes shining. "Not until you're really, really dancing!"

Jeffrey
Lynne Reid Banks

When I was ten – which was back in the 1930s, practically too long ago for even *me* to remember – my mother, a very ambitious woman, decided that what I needed was Advantages.

I see better now what she meant. I certainly needed something. I was a remarkably plain little girl, with frizzy hair and fat legs. Well, not only legs.

My mother said nothing about that. She just said that never again in my life would learning "skills" be so easy for me, and that even though I might find extra lessons "trying" now, I would thank her later.

My suspicions were instantly aroused. I had visions of dreadful things like playing bridge and flower-arranging. My mother was an acknowledged expert in both. But when I asked balefully, "Extra lessons in *what*?" she surprised me.

"Since you're getting *mental* stimulation at school – *physical* things mainly."

I at once smelt exercise. "But I hate sport!" I wailed.

My mother bridled and asked who'd said anything about sport, did I imagine she wanted me to learn football? Fencing, she added lightly, didn't count as a sport, it was more of an accomplishment.

"Fencing? What's that?"

"Fencing, darling? Well, it's – fencing. You do it with a foil." She made a few languid passes. "Very good for balance, co-ordination . . . and grace."

Before I could draw breath to argue, she had listed the other subjects she had in view. Gymnastics. Riding. And elocution.

From the next room came a cough, and the rattle of a newspaper.

"Elocution? Physical?" came my father's dry enquiry.

My mother raised her voice slightly. She disliked being challenged once she'd made up her mind.

"Perhaps I'm mistaken, but I did think the voice was of bodily origin," she remarked, as if to the air.

I had been picking myself up during this exchange, and now I exploded. "I don't want to do any of them! Mummy! PLEASE!"

My mother rode straight over my protests. She hadn't finished yet. The one thing she'd set her heart on my learning – and here her voice took on an almost mystic tone – was ballet.

I was speechless. Me? Ballet? I actually managed to burst into tears.

"Janet, darling! What's wrong with ballet?"

"The others'll laugh at me!" I didn't want to say the awful words, "I'm too fat!"

"One way to stop them laughing is to be good at it," she said firmly. "Anyway, Madame can't take you yet. Try the other things first."

The lively little lady who taught us fencing wore a

piled-up wig, and I giggled till I flopped like a ragdoll every time my partner whispered a warning against spearing it off her head with my foil.

Nevertheless, I learned how to cry *"En garde!"* and lunge to the attack, thumping my foot down (and when I thumped, the floorboards shook). I did this *all the time* at home, using everything from a school ruler to a beanpole as a foil, including among my unwilling opponents my nanny, the cook, and visitors. My grace and co-ordination didn't seem to improve, however, and my mother soon put a stop to the lessons.

I went to gymnastics about three times. I was useless. I would run at the horse and stop dead, afraid to even try to jump it. I couldn't bear to be upside-down, so I couldn't do a handstand even against a wall, let alone a cartwheel. I hated it so much I could have easily thrown up even after a simple somersault. It was my teacher who begged my mother to stop sending me.

I never even got near a real horse. I turned out to be allergic to them.

Madame at ballet still couldn't take me. So I filled in with elocution after all.

To my surprise I rather took to that. I learnt lots of soppy poems and dramatic recitations by heart, and recited them relentlessly to everyone who came to the house. This became really embarrassing for my parents.

"Will you stop her!" my father shouted at my mother. "All these expensive lessons are simply making her into an obnoxious little show-off!" In those days mothers were expected to be entirely responsible for their children's behaviour. That's why they engaged nannies, I suppose: to share the blame.

But when it came to ballet, my mother really stuck her toes in.

"She is going to do this," I heard her tell my father with a steely note in her voice. "She is going to have one Advantage, if it kills her."

"Advantage, my foot! Just because it was *your* dream—"

"That has nothing to do with it!"

So I was bought a practice dress and ballet shoes and "woolly legs" and when at last Madame had a vacancy, off I went, willy-nilly, to ballet class.

There were ten of us in mine. Nine girls and one boy. Jeffrey.

The girls teased him. I'd been teased in gymnastics so I should have learnt to be nice, but I teased him too – about having knobbly knees and about being a boy, and because his surname was Platt. We called him Pigtail.

But it's no fun teasing someone who takes no notice. Jeffrey simply wasn't concerned about anything except the lessons. He kept his head down in the changing room, and the minute he was ready he would rush to the *barre* and begin his exercises, while we girls dawdled and examined ourselves in the mirrors admiring our pretty little practice outfits, and twiddled about, pretending to be ballerinas.

Madame really had been one. I never knew which country she came from, but it certainly wasn't England. The fencing teacher had been called Madame, too, but this Madame was different. She didn't wear a wig, though her hair was greying and skimpy and pulled back from her high forehead. She didn't wear make-up or anything else that spoke of vanity. Her face was all big black snapping eyes. Her body had muscles all over like slippery fish under her thin skin, rippling and twisting. She hadn't one ounce of fat on her anywhere, and she used to look at me, not unkindly but curiously, as if I were from an alien species.

"Zhannette, dulling, you are so peellowy, I could go to sleep on you!" she used to say, marvelling, and squeeze the surplus flesh on my thigh between finger and thumb as she tried to turn my leg out from the hip. The other little girls sniggered. Of course, I knew being pillowy wasn't a good thing in a dancer. Not if dancers were supposed to look like Madame.

She was very interested in our bodies, especially our legs and feet. She used to take Jeffrey's feet in her

161

hands sometimes and turn them about as if they were pieces of fruit she wanted to buy, and then sink her teeth into. Her expression, always stern during lessons, would soften a little.

"Zheffery, you have such feet," she said more than once. "I love your feet. Make them arch. Make them point. Make them turn out. And when the time comes . . . make them jump!" Sometimes she would twist his foot slowly and strongly, until he yipped like a puppy. "I know, dulling. It hurts. I know," she said. She spoke very tenderly to him.

To the rest of us, she seldom spoke tenderly. She shouted at us, she twisted our legs mercilessly and never said sorry. She manipulated our arms and hands. She yanked our heads half off our necks if we poked our chins. And she wrenched our shoulders back, digging iron thumbs into our scapulas.

Most of the time, though, she stood in the middle of the room and screamed at us.

"Turn out! Out! OUT!" she would scream. "*That* you call a fifth position? You are no more fifth position than ducks! You stoop like old women! Look at me! I am old woman! Do I stoop and droop and turn my feet in like duck? Make your back! You have hook in your head and God hang you up from heaven!"

She clutched her head in despair so often that her wispy hair came loose and stood out like grass.

"No, no, no! Stop. Look at me. Now. Your hips

are balls and cups. Look, look my hands, this hand is ball, this hand is cup. Look how it gli-i-des . . . you can turn them out if you try, they are made for that! Swing your leg! Sweep the floor with your flat foot! NO, Zhanette. Stiff the knee, do not flop. I will *beat* you if you flop!" I was completely convinced she would.

"Zhanette! Tight your bottom, UP the head! How many times? DON'T curl so much the fingers, you are not lifting teacup! Line the arm all the way, shoulder to tip, your hand is feather, make it float!"

And then her voice would change from a crow's squawk to a croon of bliss:

"Oh, Zheffery, good the hip, good the back, up with the eyes to the fingertip, all one line, tip to toe you good boy. I will kiss you all over, I adore you!" He was probably equally sure she meant *this* threat, and would blush scarlet.

Other times, she was not so much frightening as downright embarrassing.

"Now. *Plié*. NOT SO DEEP, Zhanette. You look as if you make peepee on the lawn!"

Sometimes we got hysterical, and not only because of the funny things she said. It wasn't giggling the way we had with the fencing Madame whom we couldn't take seriously. With this Madame we were trying so hard to do what she wanted, we were so nervous of her, that we were constantly tense, which was just what she wanted us to be.

She let us giggle sometimes. But never, ever, would she let us sink down on to the ground as we had done at fencing class when the giggles got too much. Never, ever, would she let us relax until the end of the lesson. She said it was the death of dancing muscles to sit down during practice.

Our mothers or our nannies would deliver and collect us. Nowadays, the nannies would be child minders and one probably couldn't tell them apart from the mothers. But back then, you could. If only by the coats.

The mothers mostly wore fur coats, or at least fur collars or tippets. Nobody thought it was wrong in those days – it was warm and made you look posh. The nannies wore dark grey uniform coats. The mothers were usually carefully made-up and wore fancy hats with veils, and smelt of scent. The nannies wore uniform felt hats, sometimes with badges to show at which nanny-school they had qualified. They smelt of soap, and sometimes of starch and Johnson's baby powder.

There was only one exception to this firm rule. Jeffrey's mother could have been a nanny, except that her coat wasn't new enough.

"Why does Jeffrey's mummy look so poor?" I asked my nanny one day.

"Probably because she is, dear," she replied.

"If she's poor, how can she pay for the lessons?"

Nanny gave one of her sniffs.

"Funny little boy, isn't he? Fancy a boy wanting to prance around doing ballet! Not very manly."

"He's Madame's pet."

Why did I say "He's Madame's pet," in that catty way, instead of telling the truth, which was that he was by far the best dancer in the class?

One day, after I'd been going to classes for a few months, Madame gave Nanny a message, asking my mother to pick me up so she could have a word with her. I waited in the cloakroom. When my mother came back, she looked put out. No. Worse than that. She looked really upset.

"What did Madame say?" I asked anxiously.

At first she tried to get out of telling me, but I nagged until she did.

"She said you're the wrong shape for a dancer," she said shortly. She was only short with me when she was very disappointed.

I didn't say anything, but my eyes stung, and all the way home on the bus I stared out of the window, trying not to cry.

"Did she say I've got to stop?" I asked when we got home.

"No. But she said it's a waste of money." My mother was silent for a bit, and then she asked, "Do you want to stop?"

"I don't know," I almost shouted, choking back tears.

I was surprised how much I minded what Madame said about my shape. Although I'd always been very off-hand about the lessons, the truth is, the moment Madame indicated that I should give up, perversely I wanted to go on. Ballet was by far the most exciting of the extras I'd tried. In fact, I suddenly realised that ballet was the highlight of my week. The thought of never going again, never seeing Madame again, was suddenly and puzzlingly unbearable.

My mother consulted my father, who was doing the money-wasting, of course. Most fathers in those days did not consider the money they earned as belonging, even in part, to their wives, and generally had the final word about spending it. I know there was quite an argument, but in the end, Mummy came to me with a tiny winner's smile on her face.

"We've decided you should finish this term, at least. But Janet, you'll have to practise extra hard to show Madame that you deserve to stay." (". . . to show Daddy," is what I think she really meant.)

She suggested I use my bedrail as a *barre*, and made sure I spent half an hour a day practising. She wasn't Madame, and I sat down for a rest the moment her back was turned. But I practised *ronde-de-jamb-à-terres* until Nanny said I'd wear circles in the nursery lino ("And circles in my nerves as well!").

Pliés were very hard for me, but I practised till I could do them even without holding on – though I wobbled. Once I made the mistake of asking Nanny if I looked as if I were doing peepee on the lawn. She demanded to know where I'd heard such disgusting language. When I said, "From Madame," she sniffed and muttered, "Foreigners!" Nanny would never have talked about peepee. She had always taught me that talking about "vulgar" matters without using euphemisms – her euphemism for peepee was "little duties" – was irredeemably common. Or foreign, of course. It was the same thing, for Nanny.

When Madame had told Mummy she was wasting her money, what she really meant was that she, Madame, was wasting her time. Since I kept coming, she felt free to ignore me almost entirely. She didn't even pinch my thighs any more.

Some of the other girls were keen, and got quite good, but Jeffrey got better and better, and we were all very envious. He was way ahead of us and it was clear he would move up into the next class very soon.

One day we arrived and heard the piano going in the practice room. We peeped in while we changed and saw Madame coaching Jeffrey in a little solo.

None of us was ready for solos and we realised that she'd been giving him private lessons.

By this time there'd been a lot of whispering about Jeffrey's mother being poor. A girl called Nina, blessed with more curiosity than tact, actually asked him:

"How can your mother afford private lessons, Pigtail?"

Any of us, asked such a rude question, would have retorted, "Mind your own beeswax!" Jeffrey said shyly, "Madame only charges for the classes."

It's funny how I regarded people who were better than me at something. I didn't appreciate how clever or talented they were. I didn't sit there while they danced (or whatever it was they did) and think, "He is *so good* at this, I love watching him!" What I did was, I brought it all back to myself.

I stood in line sometimes, waiting for my turn to do simple *jetés* across the floor, and watched Jeffrey jumping effortlessly, his feet making no sound, his arms moving with complete assurance, exactly as Madame had shown us and which none of the rest of us could manage properly. And, instead of rejoicing in the beauty of his movements, I just thought sulkily, "How can he do that when I can't?" Or "If I was her pet I could do it like that, she just doesn't bother about me. It's not fair!"

It wasn't fair. But it was life and the distribution of talent that wasn't fair, not Madame.

One cold winter afternoon when the class ended and we were all in the child-sweat-smelling cloakroom getting dressed, we heard some kind of commotion outside in the big room. We all quietened down to listen.

We were used to hearing Madame raising her voice, but this was different. There was a note of despair in it we had never heard.

"But you cannot! You cannot! You cannot!" she cried passionately.

We exchanged looks. Then we heard another voice, a soft murmur we couldn't make out. But Jeffrey, who had been sitting on the bench putting on his outdoor shoes – heavy black lace-ups – snapped up his head like a deer hearing a shot. He jumped up. One shoe on and the other dangling from his hand by its lace, he dashed to the door of the cloakroom. We all crowded into the doorway to watch.

I wasn't surprised to see his mother, in her shabby coat and her brown felt hat, with the big unfashionable handbag she always carried, standing face-to-face with Madame who had her back to us. She was taller than Madame, but it was obvious Madame was the dominant one.

Jeffrey ran, unevenly because of the shoe but still, somehow, with a natural grace of movement, to his mother's side and took her arm. His other shoe rested on the navy blue stuff of her sleeve. It looked funny, but nobody laughed.

The other mothers, in their fur coats, and the nannies in their smart uniforms, were in the background. Some looked as if they were trying not to listen, but of course they all were.

Madame seemed beside herself. She was waving her arms. She seemed almost to be threatening Jeffrey's mother.

"You do not comprehend, Missis – what your name is? Your son has the gift. He has the arms, the back. *He has the will!* Look his feet. When have you seen such feet on a boy? You can see them once, maybe twice in a life."

Jeffrey's mother glanced down at his feet, one shod, one socked. They must have looked to her as they did to us – perfectly ordinary.

With her eyes still on the ground, she murmured, "We can't pay."

Her pale thin face flushed scarlet, and so did Jeffrey's. Some of the mothers and nannies turned their heads away as if something really unmentionable had been said.

But Madame just made it worse.

"What do I care about that!" she shrieked. "Am I a money-grubbit? I will teach him for nothing!"

The woman stiffened as if she had been insulted, and her head snapped up like Jeffrey's.

"My husband wouldn't allow that," she said, quietly but firmly. "My husband—" She stopped. Madame waited. We all waited.

Jeffrey said, "Mum!" warningly, beseechingly. But Madame's waiting silence was stronger.

"My husband never liked him coming. He doesn't think it's right for a boy to dance."

There was an awful silence. The mothers looked as if they wanted to sink through the floor to get away, but there was no escape. Madame's back was enough to show us, who knew her, that she was about to explode.

She drew in a deep breath – you could see her ribs expand; breathing in never made her shoulders rise – and said in a shrill clear voice that seemed to slide around the mirrored room and bounce off the far wall:

"Your husband is an IDIOT!"

Jeffrey's mother face went dead white. She put her arm around Jeffrey and they both turned and walked through the crowd of mothers and nannies. They drew back as if she had a contagious disease. But I thought – and yes, really, I thought this at the time – that she looked as straight and tall as if God had hung her up from heaven.

Jeffrey, in his one shoe, walked suddenly like a cripple.

There was a long, painful pause after they'd gone, and then the mothers and nannies broke from their trance of embarrassment and moved towards the cloakroom door to hurry us up and get us out of there. But something very unexpected happened.

Something – as Nanny was to say later with deep disapproval – very . . . foreign.

Madame turned to face us. She put out her arms with the fingers spread, palms backward, to keep the mothers back. And such was the command in her arms, that they all stopped.

Her face, which we had never noticed was quite old and lined, was screwed up as if in pain. Tears were running down her cheeks. She put her hands to the sides of her head and clenched all her muscles so hard she shook. She stood there absolutely silent for a moment.

And then she did the thing that got inside me and melted something cold and spoilt and selfish in me – made a difference, perhaps, to the person I was to be. Something I never forgot, and can still see in my memory now, fifty-five years later.

She reached out her arms to us, in a beautiful, uninhibited gesture of appeal.

"Come to me. Please. I need you now. Come and comfort me!"

And without hesitation, moved by a single impulse, we broke from our frozen little cluster and flowed, ran, danced, were irresistibly drawn, towards her. We clustered around her in a childish warm knot. Every one of us was moved by the desire to give her what she had flattered us by asking us for, so openly, as no grown-up had ever done in our lives.

And her arms embraced us and her tears and

kisses fell on us. Without embarrassment, but only with love, we received her loss and her sorrow, and her broken words, of which I remember only two, perhaps the saddest in the world:

"The waste! The waste!"

CURTAIN CALL
Jean Ure

When Julie and I were ten years old, we were taken to the ballet by my Aunty Vivienne. The ballet was *Giselle*, which is one of my all-time ace favourites. I always weep buckets in the second act, when the fierce avenging Wilis force poor Albrecht to dance and dance until he drops. Julie, on the other hand, always weeps buckets in Act I. It's the bit where Giselle falls down dead of a broken heart which gets her. She says it's all Albrecht's fault for deceiving her, Giselle I mean, and no doubt she is right though he was only having a bit of a flirtation. I don't think he meant her to fall in love with him.

Julie, I should tell you, is my best friend. My best *ballet* friend. Practically all my friends are ballet friends these days. I don't really have time to meet any ordinary people, but when we were ten and still only having classes twice a week, Julie was my ballet friend, and Deanne Jordan was my school friend. Deanne could never understand why I was so mad about ballet. When I left school at thirteen to go to the Dance Academy with Julie, Deanne thought I was completely loopy. She said, "You'll have to live like a *nun*." I told her that if you were dedicated it wasn't any hardship, but she just rolled her eyes and muttered about grated carrot and yoghurt, which is what she imagined I was going to have to live on for the rest of my life.

Actually I do eat quite a lot of yoghurt, and sometimes raw carrots as well, but every now and again I pig out on a Mars Bar or a plate of French fries and then spend the next two days guiltily starving myself before Madame can accuse me of getting fat. But I don't really mind. It's worth a bit of a sacrifice. There's nothing quite as thrilling as covering the stage in a series of *pirouettes* or *grands jetés*, feeling lighter than air yet strong and supple as a length of steel wire. You can't do that if you pig out too often.

Anyway. Julie and I went to see *Giselle* at the Coliseum Theatre in London. It was my birthday treat. Giselle was danced by Natalya Svetlanova, Albrecht by Gregor Dubinsky. By the end of the evening, we had both made up our minds: Julie was going to be a second Svetlanova, I was going to dance with Dubinksy.

Julie said there wasn't much chance that I ever would, considering I was only ten and Dubinsky must have been at least thirty. She said, "He'll have stopped dancing long before you're ready to be a soloist." I retorted that you can always dream.

Nothing ever changed my dream. Julie pretty soon stopped wanting to be like Natalya Svetlanova and decided she wanted to be a second Darcey Bussell instead (which she won't ever be, because (a) she is too small and (b) she is better at modern than classical). Me, I just went on dreaming that one day I would get to dance with Dubinsky.

As a matter of fact, even though he was a leading dancer and I was nobody, just a humble ballet student, and hadn't even met him, unless you count asking him for his autograph, I used privately to think of him as Gregor. I had photographs of him stuck all round my bedroom and I went to every single performance of his that I could. Fortunately, my Aunty Vivienne, whom Julie and I lived with while we were at the Academy, was also mad about him and she quite often used to get free tickets for us – for her and me and Julie. This is because she knew someone who worked backstage at the theatre where he appeared, which wasn't the Coliseum any more but the Royal Garden, which is the home of the Royal Garden Ballet. Gregor was now their big star!

But he was also getting quite old. One Christmas when I was fourteen, we went to see him in the *Nutcracker* and I felt really angry because a stupid idiotic woman sitting behind us remarked to her companion that "Dubinsky's going to be past it quite soon. He'll be forty next year, you know." So what? He could still dance! Rudolf Nureyev, who was another great Russian dancer, went on until he was well past forty.

Julie said, "Yes, but lots of people say he shouldn't have done." And then she added, teasingly, "If you're going to dance with Dubinsky, you'd better get a move on!"

She wouldn't have teased me, I don't think, if she'd realised how utterly *passionately* I dreamed of dancing with Gregor. I didn't just have a teenage crush on him. To dance with Gregor Dubinsky was the whole aim and purpose of my life. It was what kept me going during the long-drawn-out torture of Madam's early morning classes. It was what gave me hope, and strength, and determination. When my feet were sore and bleeding, or every muscle in my body cried out in protest – "We can't go on!" – it was that will o' the wisp light at the end of the tunnel which made me endure.

I expect that one day, when I am a famous ballerina (I suppose that here I ought modestly to add "Ha ha" or "Some hopes" but I truly do believe that one day I *will* be), I expect that I will write my autobiography, and in it I will tell how I fulfilled my childhood ambition: how I danced with the great Russian *premier danseur*, Gregor Dubinsky. And when I write it, no one will believe me.

No one who knows about ballet, that is. They will accuse me, in all probability, of making it up.

"How can she have danced with Dubinsky?" they will scoff. "She was only fifteen when he died!"

They will go back and consult their programmes (because people who are balletomanes quite often keep programmes going back for decades). They will find the one which gives details of the very first performance of Gregor's ballet, *Light of the World*. They will know (because they always know this sort of thing) that it was in *Light of the World* that I made my debut – my first performance on the professional stage. And they will look down the cast list, just to check, in case their memories have played them false, and they will seize triumphantly upon the fact that Gregor did not appear in his own ballet. He was scheduled to do so, but he never did. A dancer called Michael Hammond took the part that Gregor should have danced.

The reason Michael took over Gregor's role was that Gregor was in hospital. He died that same night; so how could I possibly have danced with him?

"She couldn't! She's making it up!"

But I'm not making it up. I *did* dance with him – and I don't just mean in rehearsal. I danced on stage with Gregor Dubinsky!

This is how it happened. When I was fifteen, I was promoted to be one of Madame's "specials" – an honour, but one she certainly made you pay for. Sometimes I could hardly crawl out of bed in the morning for the creaking and aching of my joints. Lots of ballet dancers are permanently crippled by the time they are middle-aged, which only confirms my friend Deanne in her view that we are all stark mad. Maybe it is true: ballet does make highly unnatural demands on the human body. I mean, for instance, feet are not *designed* to turn out at right angles from each other, nor hips to be rotated in their sockets. I have to admit that there is a lot of pain and suffering involved. "Self-mutilation" Deanne calls it with a sniff. But the rewards make it all worth it!

I think Gregor would have agreed with that, even though it was dancing which killed him. He suffered from blood clots in his legs and ought by rights to have retired years before, but he couldn't bring himself to do so. He loved dancing too much! He just couldn't imagine life without it. And neither can I.

Although it was the most terrible tragedy when Gregor died (we all of us sobbed, even including Madame), the one consolation, as Aunty Vivienne said, was that "he died in harness", meaning that he actually collapsed while on stage. I do think that is a better way for a dancer to go than lingering on for years being forced to watch other people, though Deanne says that when I am "forty and past it" I will feel quite differently.

We shall see! The way I feel at the moment, I cannot believe this to be true.

After I'd been one of Madame's specials for about two months, there was a great buzz in the Academy because Gregor, whom most people called "Maestro", was rumoured to be putting on a new ballet for which he needed students from the Academy.

For a long time it remained just a rumour, then one day a girl called Ellen Tomkins (Tomkins! What a name for a dancer!) read in a magazine that "Gregor Dubinsky is making a new ballet on Rosemary Alexander, prima ballerina of the Royal Garden." The ballet was to be called *Light of the World* and Alexander would be partnered, as usual, by Raul Ordoñez. Dubinsky himself would be dancing the small but important role of The Maker.

Such excitement! If it were true that a new ballet was being rehearsed, then who knew? It might also be true that some of us would be picked to appear in it!

And indeed, Madame confirmed the very next day that the Maestro would shortly be visiting us to pick out half a dozen advanced students to take the part of children. She explained that these were *dancing* roles, which was why advanced students were required, but that as we were to be children it would obviously be the smallest ones who stood most chance of being chosen.

Julie preened at this, but my heart sank, because although I am not tall I am not particularly tiny. There were several other students shorter than me.

The great day came, and the Maestro strode into the studio with Madam teetering behind him on her high heels. (She wears these huge heels to make herself appear more intimidating. In reality she is even more minute than Julie who is practically a *midget*.)

The Maestro – we all had to call him this, and so

I started in the end to think of him in that way – was wearing black slacks and a black sweater. He was also smoking! It is very bad for dancers to smoke, but lots of them do. I am never going to. Someone said later that if Maestro hadn't smoked he might not have had these blood clots in his legs. I don't know whether this is true or not.

Although he was over forty now, he was still what Aunty Vivienne calls "a strikingly attractive man". By this she means that he had these high Russian cheekbones with slanting Slavic eyes and very thick black hair, which was *not* dyed. I know this for a fact, because when you got close you could see that there were just the odd one or two silver strands amongst the black. If he had dyed it, there wouldn't have been. It stands to reason.

It was Madame who took the class. The Maestro sat on a high stool and watched, through narrowed eyes and a haze of cigarette smoke. (He is the *only* person Madame would have allowed to smoke in one of her classes. But I suppose when you are famous you can get away with anything.)

I think the following hour was one of the most punishing I have ever been put through. It was like Madame was showing us off, demonstrating just how far she could push us. We all survived – just about - but Julie did say afterwards that she was seriously beginning to wonder "whether it was all worth it". I was quite shocked, actually. It made me realise, for the first time, that there was a serious difference in outlook between Julie and me. I felt drained after Madame's class, but exhilarated, too. Of course it was worth it!

To cut a long story short, because quite honestly the next twenty-four hours felt more like twenty-fours days, both Julie and I were chosen – and I was singled out to dance a *real named part*! I was to be "The Child of the Future" and have a whole *pas de deux* with the Maestro!

I learnt later – a lot later – that Madame and the Maestro had had quite an argument about this. The Maestro's choreography was always very inventive, very acrobatic and a bit tricksy, and Madame reckoned that what he was asking me to do was something beyond my capabilities. She wanted him to cast the part from within the ranks of the Company, but the Maestro dug his heels in. He shouted (I got this from someone who overheard him and Madame going at it hammer and tongs in Madame's office), "I want little blonde!"

That was me! *I* was the little blonde. And I was going to dance with the great Dubinsky!

"*Well*," said Julie, as we went back to Aunty Vivienne's after Madame had made the announcement, "whoever would have thought it? All those years ago, when we saw him in *Giselle* . . . and here you are, being partnered by him!"

I was dead nervous at first, not just because of

dancing with my hero but also because I secretly feared, like Madame, that some of the technical demands might be too much for me. There was one lift, in particular, that scared me almost paralytic. I had to do a dive – what is called a fish dive – then at the last minute, with help from the Maestro, rotate very quickly, round and up, so that I ended high in the air, bending out backwards to the audience. To make it even more scary, I had to take the initial leap from the top of a rostrum. It meant launching myself into space and trusting blindly to the Maestro.

He knew that it terrified me. He was very patient; very caring and coaxing. In his rolling Russian accent, which he never managed to lose, he used to assure me that "No problem! Not to be frightened to dance with old man. He catch. OK! Hop-là!" And then, as I felt his broad strong hands supporting me: "Not so bad, eh, Ninotchka?"

My name is Ninette. Ninotchka was his way of making it sound Russian. No one else has ever, ever called me Ninotchka. Only the Maestro.

All the others were so envious of me! They kept wanting to know, "What is it like, dancing with Dubinsky?" I could only tell them that it was bliss. Pure bliss! I felt so safe, and also tremendously *special*. My part was only tiny, but he gave me as much time and attention as if I'd been a major soloist. And he was kind! Not in the least bit grand or patronising, though I'd heard members of the

Company say that he could be. He had a reputation for throwing tantrums, but with me he was unfailingly gentle and considerate. Oh, how I loved him!

And then there came that terrible night. The Company were putting on a triple bill, *Sylphides*, *Petrushka* and *Les Patineurs*, the lovely skating ballet. I was there, watching, up in the gods with Julie, when it happened. One minute the Maestro was spinning, in a whirl of snowflakes: the next he was in a crumpled heap on the floor.

At first we thought he must have slipped, must have lost his balance or maybe pulled a muscle. It wasn't until later that we heard the terrible truth: the Maestro was in hospital, unconscious, and it was feared he might never recover.

The premiere of his ballet was due the next day. There was some talk of cancelling, but we all knew that that was not what he would have wanted. For him, "the show must go on" was not just an empty phrase: he had danced many, many times in great pain from injury. So Michael Hammond took over his role and Madame fitted in an extra rehearsal specially for him and me because she was so worried about that one particular lift and whether I would be able to cope. Michael had understudied the part, but he was no Maestro. He was terrified, and so was I. I knew he thought that I was too young and inexperienced, and without the Maestro to cast his magic I was almost beginning to think so myself. (Madame told me later that she had actually considered replacing me with a member of the Company. The only reason she hadn't done so was that "You were the Maestro's choice: he wanted you above anyone else.")

And so the show went on. The Child of the Future didn't appear until almost the very end, which meant I had the whole evening in which to imagine the worst. Suppose Michael didn't catch me? Suppose my nerve gave way? Suppose I let the Maestro down?

For the first few dreadful minutes after my entrance I really feared that I might be going to. I couldn't dance with Michael! I didn't trust him enough! He just didn't inspire me with confidence.

And then came the moment – the moment I had been dreading: the fish dive off the rostrum. And I knew I couldn't do it!

Then it was that the miracle occurred. I heard a voice that whispered "OK! Hop-là!" Obedient to its command, I launched myself into space. The hands that caught and held me were broad and strong. The voice that encouraged me had a rolling Russian accent: "Not so bad, eh, Ninotchka?"

I danced as well as I had ever danced with the Maestro – because, of course, I *was* dancing with him. Madame stood in the wings, nodding and

beaming. Julie gave me the thumbs-up. But Michael, looking completely dazed as we took our bow, could only mutter, "What happened? Did we do it?"

He couldn't even remember being on stage! He said that "Someone – or something – seemed to take over. I just blanked out!" He was desperate to know if it had been all right. It was Madame who reassured him. She said, "You took on the mantle of the Maestro. He would have been proud of you!"

The curtain came down at ten minutes past ten. At a quarter past, we heard later, the Maestro departed this life.

At least he waited for his curtain call. I just hope he heard the applause . . .

AFTERWORD

Many young dancers dream of performing on a famous stage – pretending to become a fairy-tale character, a prince, Cinderella or Alice in Wonderland for a few hours. They imagine listening to the ballet music, dancing the steps, wearing the magical costumes and hearing the swish of the heavy velvet curtain as they step out to take their curtain call to receive the congratulatory bouquets.

The demands of becoming a dancer involve long, physically tough training, but they have never deterred the dedicated young dancer. The rewards come from perseverance, a good attitude, musicality and a sound training. This imaginative children's book reflects the passion that most dancers feel, and will undoubtedly encourage the talented young dancer. I hope that many children will enjoy this book and will be inspired by it.

Jill Tookey
Founder and Artistic Director
National Youth Ballet of Great Britain

THE NATIONAL YOUTH BALLET
OF GREAT BRITAIN

The National Youth Ballet, whose patrons include Darcey Bussell, Principal Dancer with the Royal Ballet, devises innovative ballets for children, often with specially commissioned music. Its aim is to involve talented young dancers in all aspects of creating a ballet – from the conception of an idea through to a performance on stage.

Young dancers, who audition from all over Great Britain, are taught by professional choreographers and have the opportunity to meet the costumiers and the composers as well as learn about the sets and how to apply theatrical make-up.

Many former NYB dancers are now with professional companies, having been given invaluable performing experience, confidence and insight behind the scenes.

The NYB also hold popular workshops offering hundreds more children a wonderful opportunity to enjoy the magic and joy of dance.

If you would like to know more, please write to:

The National Youth Ballet of Great Britain
The Pheasantry
Vicarage Hall
Westerham
Kent
TN16 1AY